HOLIDAY HULLABALOO!

HOLIDAY HULLABALOO!

FACTS, JOKES, AND RIDDLES

BY E. RICHARD CHURCHILL
with Eric and Sean Churchill

Designed by Nicholas Krenitsky

Franklin Watts/New York/London/1977

Library of Congress Cataloging in Publication Data

Churchill, Elmer Richard.
Holiday hullabaloo!

Includes index.
SUMMARY: A discussion of holidays in the United States accompanied by jokes and riddles appropriate to each holiday.
1. Holidays—United States—Juvenile literature. 2. Wit and humor, Juvenile. [1. Holidays. 2. Joke books. 3. Riddles] I. Title.
GT3933.C48 394.2'6973 76-39909
ISBN 0-531-00384-1

Printed in the United States of America
5 4 3

Contents

New Year's Day 1
Benjamin Franklin's Birthday 8
Groundhog Day 15
Boy Scout Day 20
Lincoln's Birthday 29
Saint Valentine's Day 36
Washington's Birthday 44
Girl Scout Day 53
Saint Patrick's Day 61
April Fool's Day 67
Easter 78
Arbor Day 86
May Day 91
Mother's Day 96
Children's Day 101
Flag Day 109
Father's Day 115
Independence Day 122
Labor Day 127
Columbus Day 145
Halloween 153
Thanksgiving 164
Christmas 169

HOLIDAY HULLABALOO!

New Year's Day

The celebration of New Year's Day dates back to prehistoric times. As early as 4241 B.C. the ancient Egyptians celebrated their new year when the Nile River flooded in July. The ancient Greeks celebrated the festival on the first full moon after June 21. In ancient Britain, the Druids held their celebration on March 10 and passed around branches of mistletoe to ensure a good New Year.

March 25, the time of the vernal or spring equinox, was a common time of celebration for many people over a number of years. In 46 B.C., with the development of the Julian calendar, the Romans set January 1 as New Year's Day. Even so, it wasn't until the calendar change in 1582 that January 1 was commonly celebrated as New Year's Day.

The calendars of the world have been changed time and again. People have tried to perfect a calendar that fits their needs and keeps pace with the seasons. Julius Caesar, for example, added leap year to the calendars in 45 B.C. in an effort to make the calendar more accurate. With each calendar change the day for the celebration of the new year was likely to change. Thus New Year's Day has moved about quite a bit over the years.

Since ancient times, New Year's has been a celebration involving change, beginning anew, and considerable partying. Our present custom of blowing horns and spinning noisemakers is an old one. The Chinese long ago clanged cymbals and used firecrackers to drive off the evil forces of darkness. People of many nations ring church bells to welcome in the new year. The people of Scotland used to get rid of the old year by burning a dummy representing the year just past. Several other places either buried or drowned a straw dummy of the old year.

The custom of wearing masks during this holiday celebration has been with us for years. Today a masked ball is about the only carry-over of this custom, since we leave masks for Halloween. People have been exchanging gifts on New Year's Day since Roman times. From then until the Middle Ages the giving of gifts to rulers was a custom in some lands. In Italy, children are now given gifts of money; and in Greece, Saint Basil brings gifts, which are put in children's shoes. At midnight the children get up to open their presents and welcome the new year.

In ancient Babylon the time of the new year was one for predicting what the year ahead was to bring. For many people of various nations the days just before New Year's Day were thought to be a sign of the way the coming year was to go. In some parts of England young boys called Howlers beat the fruit trees to cause them to bear a good crop in the coming year.

Starting the new year in good form has long been an important part of the day. For many this meant all debts were to be repaid by New Year's Day. For others it became a time of change. Resolutions were made that were intended to help the person lead a better life during the coming year.

The American observance of New Year's dates back to the native Americans. For some tribes the new year began after the harvest was in. It was the Iroquois Indians who began their new year sometime between January and March. Here, again, masks were used in the celebration. For the Iroquois this became a time for forgiving past sins and allowing each person to begin the new year in a better manner.

The early settlers in the New World brought their customs with them. For many these included parties and drinking as part of the celebration. Some colonial families held open house on New Year's and laid out great feasts for all who cared to stop. Another custom was that of holding a watch-night service to greet the new year. Instead of firecrackers, pistols were often used to welcome in the coming year. George Washington began the custom of holding a reception for high officials while he was President.

Naturally some interesting superstitions are a part of this holiday. A new calendar should not be put up before New Year's Day. If you are the first to drink from a well, you will have a lucky year. If red clouds show on New Year's morning, there will be much trouble and crime that year. If you work on New Year's Day, you will have a year of hard work. If the day is calm, the summer will be dry; but if a strong wind blows, there will be floods that spring.

If your first visitor on New Year's Day is a woman, bad luck will follow. If it is a man, you will have good luck. The people of Scotland believed that a dark-haired man brought good luck. For this reason they used to hire dark-haired men to be the first to set foot inside the doors of the community on New Year's Day. This was called first-footing. If the first-footer brought food, that was all the better, but it was bad luck to take anything out of the house without bringing something in. It also brought bad luck if you left the house before someone else had arrived.

The English drank from a wassail bowl on New Year's Eve. In it was a ring. If an unmarried person caught the ring in the ladle, that person would marry during the coming year. The French eat pancakes to bring good luck for the year, and the Germans eat fish for the same reason. The people of Switzerland let a drop of cream fall on the floor to guarantee abundance.

Today's New Year's Day celebration in the United States seems to center around the fabulous Tournament of Roses parade and the countless football "bowl" games. It is still a time for resolutions and reflections, however, and a hope for a good year to come.

Why is a New Year's resolution like last week's trash?

The quicker it is carried out the better.

Spineless Sam made New Year's resolutions year after year and broke them all. Finally, one New Year's Day he told his family he had made a resolution he was certain he could keep.

"What is that?" asked his unbelieving wife.

"To stop making New Year's resolutions," Sam replied happily.

Just before the stroke of midnight, one New Year's Eve partygoer turned to another and asked, "Will you join me in a drink?"

The other hesitated for a minute, then replied, "If you're sure there is room enough for the two of us."

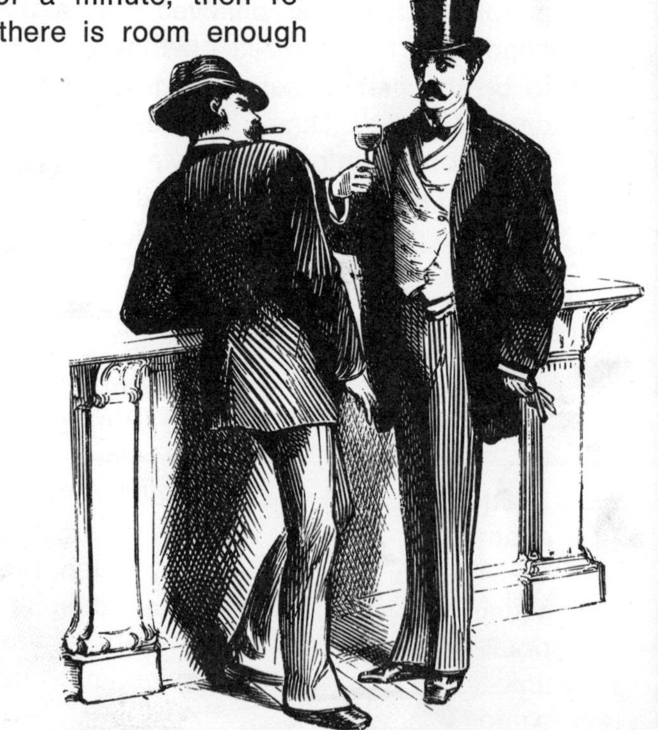

Drab Dora came home from the New Year's Eve party in tears.

"What's wrong?" asked her mother.

"At midnight they awarded a prize for the most clever mask and I won," said Dora.

"What is so bad about that?" her mother demanded.

"I wasn't wearing a mask," Dora moaned.

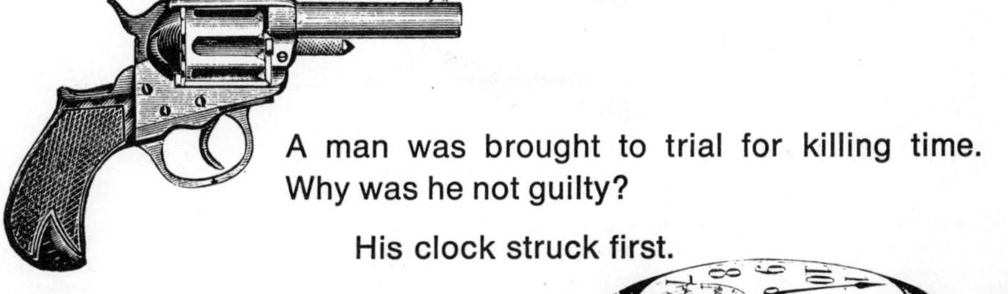

A man was brought to trial for killing time. Why was he not guilty?

His clock struck first.

Wife who is dressing for a New Year's Eve party, to her impatient husband: "For heaven's sake, stop fidgeting. I've been telling you for an hour that I'll be ready in a minute."

"Now don't lose your head at the party tonight," the nagging wife cautioned her husband.

"I wouldn't think of it, dear," the poor fellow replied. "If I did, I would have no place to carry my hat."

Why was the fellow hurt when his friends threw a large party New Year's Eve?

He was the large party they threw.

The man had paid a fortune for nightclub tickets on New Year's Eve. As the evening dragged on, he became more and more unhappy with the poor floor show. Finally he left his table and walked over to the head waiter. Drawing a revolver, he said, "I don't like the floor show. Give me everybody's money back!"

Pat: "What a New Year's Eve I had. I spent it with the biggest spender in town."

Mike, much impressed: "And who might that have been?"

Pat, with sadness: "My wife."

Why is the calendar sad on New Year's Eve?

Because its days are numbered.

Said Talking Tilly to her friend, "My New Year's resolution is not to repeat gossip, so make sure you listen carefully the first time!"

Why did the man put his clock on the stove on the night of December 31?

He wanted to have a hot time on New Year's Eve.

The invited guest forgot all about the swinging New Year's Eve party to which he had been invited. Full of remorse, he phoned the hostess to apologize. After making his apology he awaited her reply.

"Oh," she said at last, "weren't you there?"

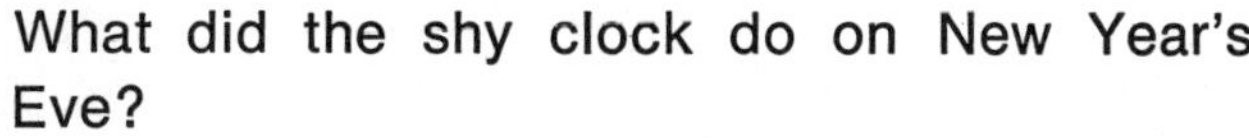

What did the shy clock do on New Year's Eve?

It kept its hands in front of its face.

What did the watch's minute hand say to the hour hand on New Year's Eve?

I'll be around in an hour.

A husband was in the kitchen cleaning up after the New Year's Eve party. Suddenly his wife in the living room heard a tremendous crash.

"Oh, no!" she cried. "More of my best glasses?"

"Nope," her husband called back. "Less."

What is apt to be the most dangerous part of a car on New Year's Eve?

The nut behind the wheel.

Franklin's Birthday

The first celebration of Benjamin Franklin's birthday was held in Boston in 1826, by the Franklin Typographical Society. This group of printers has continued to celebrate the birthday of the famous printer, inventor, and statesman ever since. Another famous group honoring Franklin's birthday is the Poor Richard Club in Philadelphia. Also in Philadelphia is the largest building dedicated to Ben Franklin. It is the Franklin Institute, which was built in 1934. This huge building cost $3 million to build and houses a museum of mechanics and a planetarium.

Benjamin Franklin was born January 17, 1706, in Boston, Massachusetts. He was the fifteenth child in a family of seventeen. After two years in school, Ben was kept home by his father to help in the family candle and soap business.

When Ben was twelve he became an apprentice to his older brother James, who was a printer. It was while Ben was learning the printing trade from his brother that he secretly wrote several articles for the paper and signed them "Mrs. Silence Dogood." When Ben was seventeen he ran away to Philadelphia, the largest city in the colonies. His first purchase in that great city was three loaves of bread, which he ate as he walked down the street.

Ben worked for several printers until he bought his own print shop in 1730. From then until 1766 he published *The Pennsylvania Gazette.* From 1733 until 1758 he also wrote and published *Poor Richard's Almanac,* which is best remembered for its wise sayings. Some of Franklin's best-remembered sayings include:

> God helps those that help themselves.
>
> A penny saved is a penny earned.
>
> Early to bed and early to rise, makes a man healthy, wealthy, and wise.
>
> An ounce of prevention is worth a pound of cure.
>
> He who falls in love with himself will have no rivals.

Franklin's accomplishments were many. As postmaster of Philadelphia he did much to improve colonial mail service and started the first dead-letter office. He set up the world's first public library and organized a fire department. He started a program to pave and light the city streets. America's first city hospital was his idea, as was an academy that became the University of Pennsylvania.

As a scientist he worked with electricity and invented the lightning rod to protect buildings. Once Ben tried to electrocute a turkey and almost killed himself. He said, "I meant to kill a turkey, and instead, I nearly killed a goose."

Ben suggested daylight saving time for summer, invented a metal stove and bifocal glasses, studied the Gulf Stream, and learned to use lime to improve some soils. However, he never got a patent on any of his inventions. Franklin said his discoveries should be for the good of everyone.

About the time of the French and Indian War, Ben became active in politics. In 1757 he was sent to London to represent the colonies and stayed there during much of the next eighteen years.

In 1775, he became postmaster general for all the colonies. He helped write the Declaration of Independence and was one of its signers. Later, in 1776, he went to France, where he worked to convince France to help the colonists fight Britain. In 1783 he helped write and signed the treaty that ended the Revolutionary War.

Soon after Franklin returned to America he became a member of the Constitutional Convention. It was his idea to have both a Senate and House of Representatives to write the laws. A few years later he was elected president of America's first antislavery society.

Franklin died April 17, 1790, at the age of eighty-four. Over 20,000 mourners attended his funeral, which says much about the feeling Americans held for Benjamin Franklin.

What did Ben Franklin decide was the big difference between lightning and electricity?

No matter how much inflation raises the cost of electricity, lightning is still free.

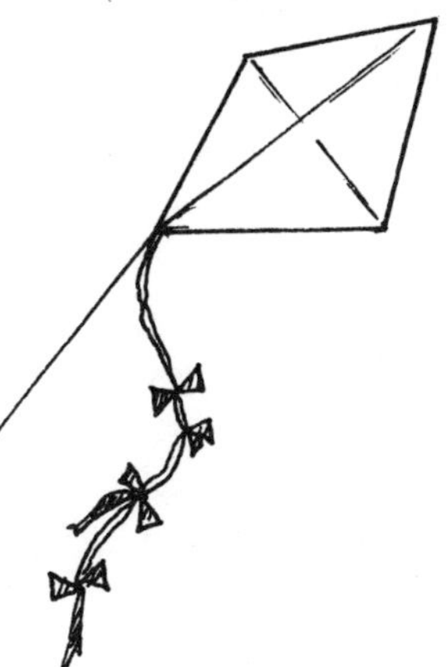

What sort of paper did Ben Franklin use for his famous kite experiment?

Fly paper.

What did Ben Franklin say when he discovered that lightning was electricity?

"My, what a shocking discovery!"

What happened when Ben fell into his bifocal lens grinding machine?

He nearly made a spectacle of himself.

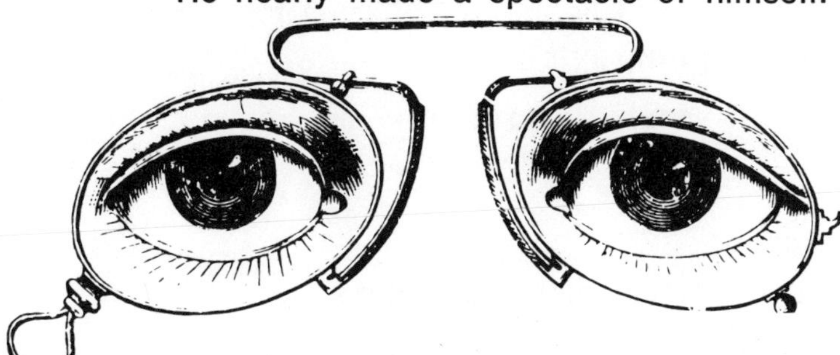

At what time in his life was Ben Franklin a conductor?

When his kite was struck by lightning.

Lloyd to Floyd: "Where was Franklin born?"

"Boston," replied Floyd.

"What part?" wondered Lloyd.

"Why, all of him, I suppose," answered Floyd.

Why did Ben Franklin's mother call him sonny?

Because he was so bright.

What fruit is found on a Franklin half-dollar?

A date.

What did Ben say when the doctor told him the pain in his left leg was caused by old age?

"Nonsense! It is the same age as my right leg."

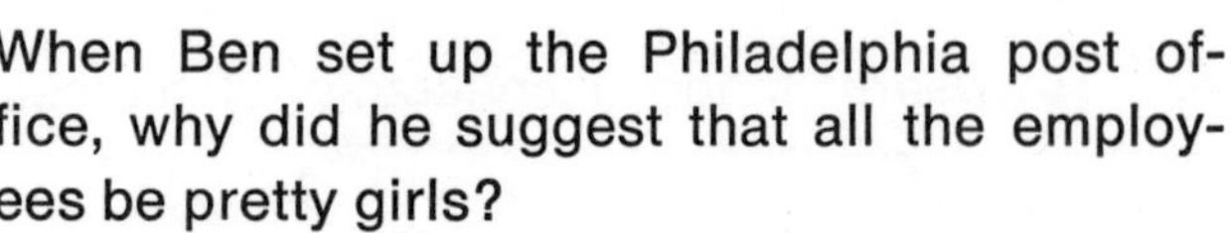

When Ben set up the Philadelphia post office, why did he suggest that all the employees be pretty girls?

It would keep the mails coming and going constantly.

Why did Ben Franklin become a printer?

He just seemed to be the right type.

How did Ben Franklin know the first public library was burning?

He saw volumes of smoke.

Teacher: "Just remember what Franklin said. 'Early to bed and early to rise, makes a man healthy, wealthy, and wise.' "

Student: "Even if you are a night watchman?"

Though Franklin's inventions are pretty well known, few people know that he once crossed honey bees and lightning bugs so the bees could see to work in the dark.

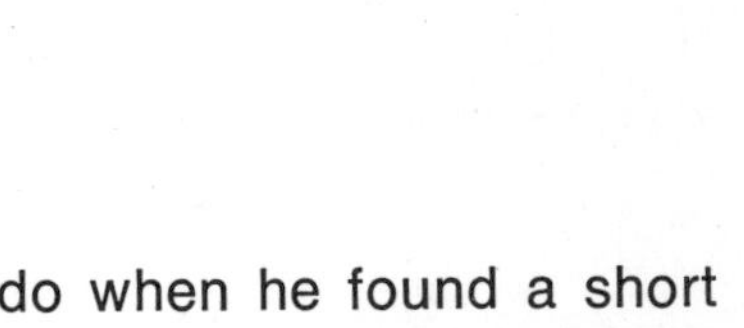

What did Franklin do when he found a short circuit in one of his electrical experiments?

He lengthened it.

When Ben was experimenting one day, he discovered a liquid that did not freeze. What was it?

Boiling water.

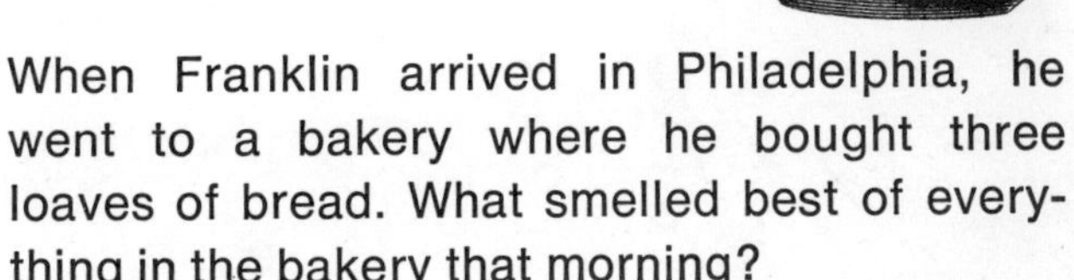

When Franklin arrived in Philadelphia, he went to a bakery where he bought three loaves of bread. What smelled best of everything in the bakery that morning?

Ben's nose.

Everyone knows of Ben Franklin's experiments with electricity, but exactly where was he when the lights went out?

In the dark.

What building did Franklin cause to be the tallest in Philadelphia?

The library Ben established had the most stories of any building.

Little Joe told his parents the people of Philadelphia weren't as smart now as when Franklin had lived there.

"How can that be?" his mother demanded.

"Well," Joe defended himself, "it must be true, because I read it in a book. It said the population of Philadelphia is much denser now than at the time of Franklin."

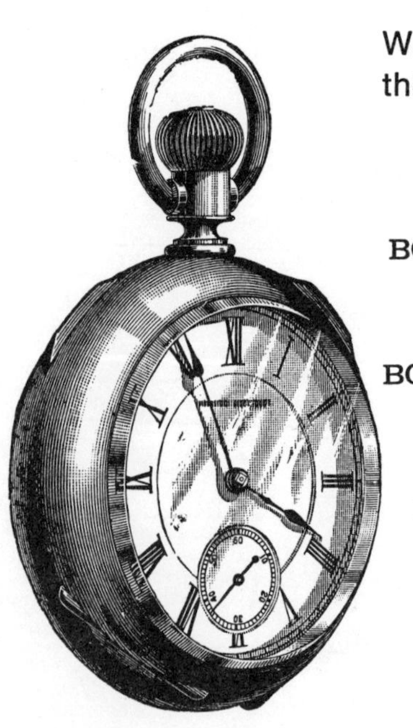

What time was it when Ben's clock struck thirteen?

Time for Ben to quit experimenting with his clock.

BONG. . . .

BONG. . . . BONG. . . .

BONG. . . .

BONG. . . .

BONG. . . . BONG. . . .

BONG. . . . BONG. . . . BONG. . . .

BONG. . . . BONG. . . .

BONG.

Groundhog Day

As far back as the Middle Ages, farmers looked to animals as weather predictors. It was believed that hibernating animals chose February 2 to come out of their dens and check weather conditions.

When settlers from Germany moved to Pennsylvania, they brought this belief with them. In Germany, however, they depended on the badger to predict the coming weather. Since badgers weren't common where they settled in Pennsylvania, the groundhog became a substitute.

According to tradition, if the groundhog comes out of its burrow on Groundhog Day and sees its shadow, there will be six more weeks of winter. If, however, the day is cloudy and the groundhog can't see its shadow, then it is safe for the farmers to plant their crops.

Several old rhymes say the same thing.

If Candlemas Day be fair and clear,
  There'll be five winters in the year.

Incidentally, Candlemas is February 2. Another rhyme says:

If Candlemas be fair and bright,
  Winter will have another flight;
But if it is dark with clouds and rain,
  Winter is gone and will not come again.

Interestingly enough, in some areas Groundhog Day used to be celebrated on February 14, the same as Saint Valentine's Day. It was believed that on this day the birds and animals chose their mates for the coming spring.

As early as 1898 groundhog societies were formed in the United States. Most of them are in Pennsylvania and are devoted to fun and good humor. Some of these societies or clubs claim *their* own favorite groundhog is the most accurate in predicting the coming weather. However, the National Geographic Society studied the situation and says that the groundhog is only right about one out of every three times.

Being right one out of three isn't all that good, but the National Weather Service isn't right all the time either!

What is the difference between a groundhog and a flea?

A groundhog can have fleas, but a flea can't have groundhogs.

How do groundhogs usually find the weather on Groundhog Day?

By going outside.

Why did the groundhog keep scratching himself?

He was the only one who knew where it itched.

Which side of a groundhog has the most fur?

The outside.

What do they call groundhogs in Texas?

Groundhogs.

How is an elephant like a groundhog?

Neither one can operate an electric can opener.

What happened when they crossed a groundhog with a tiger?

When it gives a weather prediction, *everybody* listens.

Why did the spider spin a web across the groundhog's doorway?

It couldn't knit.

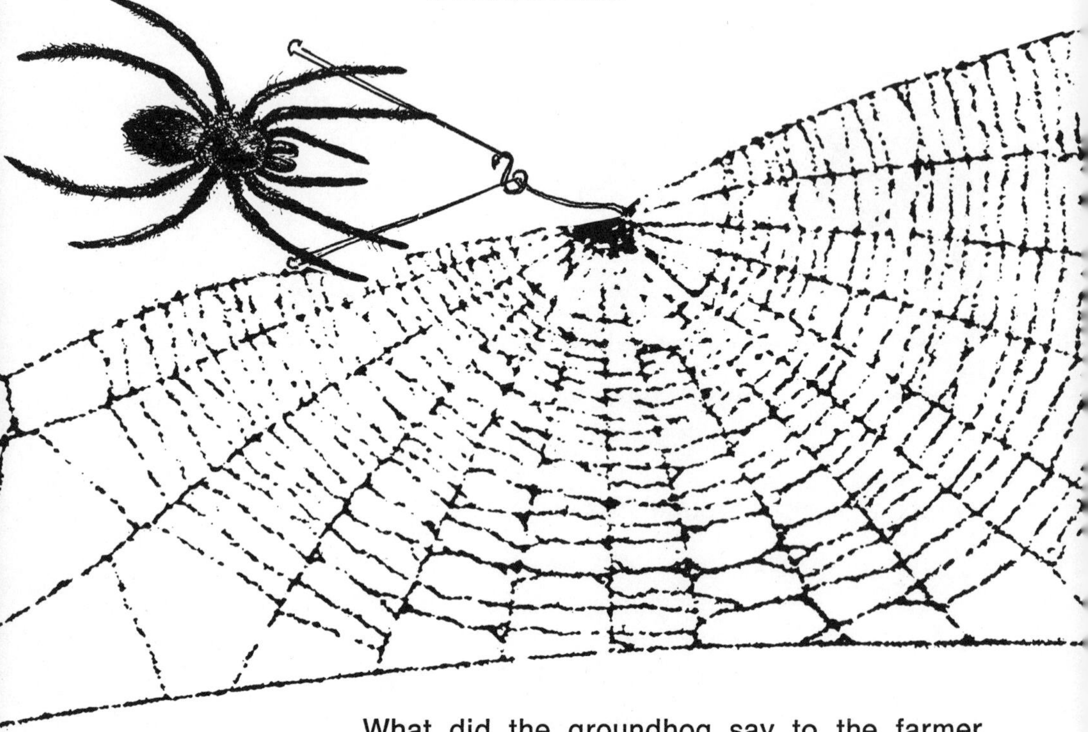

What did the groundhog say to the farmer when it saw its shadow?

Nothing. Groundhogs can't talk.

Son: "What do groundhogs do all winter?"

Dad: "They sleep."

Son: "What if they can't sleep?"

Dad: "Then they do something else."

Mother groundhog saw her son frantically chasing his tail. "Whatever are you doing, Junior?" she demanded.

"Trying to make both ends meet," Junior replied.

What is the difference between a groundhog and an elephant?

A groundhog can sit on an elephant, but an elephant should never sit on a groundhog.

How many legs would a groundhog have if you call its tail a leg?

Four. Calling something by another name doesn't make it that.

What do groundhogs have that no other animal has?

Baby groundhogs.

What happened to the groundhog who stayed up all night to see where the sun came from?

It finally dawned on him.

What sort of tree does a groundhog sit under when it rains on Groundhog Day?

A wet one.

Boy Scout Day

February 8, 1910, was the day the Boy Scouts of America received their charter. However, that was not the actual beginning of the Boy Scouts. Two years before, in Britain, the first Boy Scout group had been formed. A British army officer named Sir Robert Baden-Powell wrote a book called *Aids to Scouting*. This book was used as a guide to building character in boys. His first scout troop had only seven or eight boys in it, but its membership soon grew.

After Sir Robert Baden-Powell began working with his Boy Scouts the idea spread quickly. The year the program began in Britain an American publisher, Mr. William D. Boyce, was lost in a London fog. A boy scout helped him find his way. When the publisher offered to pay, the boy refused his money. "A boy scout never accepts money for doing a good deed," the boy told him.

The American was at once interested in the scouting program. He soon met the founder of the program and learned how it worked. When Mr. Boyce returned to the United States he brought the idea with him.

When the Boy Scouts of America began in 1910, the President of the United States was made the honorary head of the scouts. This custom has continued. Several other groups that were much like the scouts joined the organization in its early days, which helped give the program a good start.

In 1930 the Cub Scouts were added to give younger boys a chance to get into the program. For older scouts an Explorer program has been added as well. Today over 6 million boys and men take part in the scouting program in the United States.

Boy scouting is now carried on in over eighty nations of the world. This wide interest in scouting makes the program one way of bringing the world's peoples together.

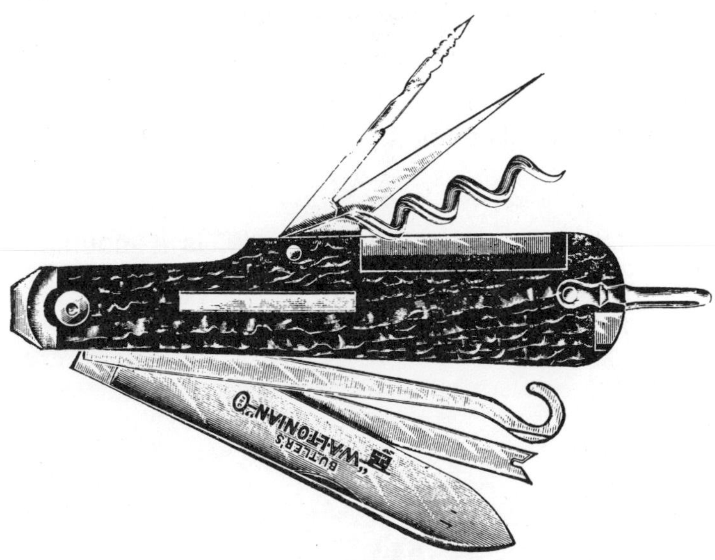

The two scouts were crossing a log bridge when one fell in. His friend immediately dived into the water and saved the lad. Later the scoutmaster said, "That was a brave thing to do, John."

"I didn't have any choice," John replied. "He had my new knife in his pocket."

Did you hear about the little scout who was chased by a bear in his pajamas? Just how the bear got into his pajamas is something of a mystery, of course.

What time was it when the little scout met an angry lion?

Time to be somewhere else.

What is the easiest way for a boy scout to start a fire with two sticks?

Make sure one of the sticks is a match.

When can a scout have an empty pocket in his uniform yet still have something in his pocket?

When he has a hole in his pocket.

Scoutmaster: "What, exactly, is a mountain range?"

Tenderfoot: "A stove for high-altitude cooking, sir."

When a boy scout loses something, why does he always find it in the last place he looks?

Because he stops looking for it as soon as he finds it.

Did you hear about the scout who went lion-hunting with only a club? Of course, there were sixty-four people in the hunting club he went with.

What did the boy scout say to the old lady before crossing the busy street?

"To avoid that run-down feeling, look both ways before crossing."

A boy scout and his brother had just rescued a lady's kitten. When she offered a reward, the scout said regretfully, "I'm sorry, but I'm a boy scout. I can't take a reward for doing a good deed."

As the woman turned away, he added quickly, "But my little brother isn't a scout. He could accept a reward."

If a boy scout crawled into a hole bored clear through the earth, where would he finally come out?

Out of the hole.

Eagle scout: "Wow! We just saw fresh bear tracks south of camp."

Tenderfoot: "Quick, which way is north?"

What kind of umbrella does a boy scout carry on a rainy day?

A wet one.

Scout: "Is it true that a mountain lion won't hurt you if you carry a flashlight?"

Troop leader: "It all depends on how fast you carry it."

The older scout was telling about his escape from a bear in Yellowstone. "There I was, running like mad for the only tree around. The bottom branch was thirty feet from the ground. I leaped for it, but I missed it."

Tenderfoot: "Wow, what happened then?"

Older Scout: "Oh, it worked out all right. I caught it coming down!"

How would you divide nine potatoes equally among seven hungry boy scouts?

Mash them first.

Why was the scoutmaster upset to find the troop sitting before a blazing fire in his recreation room?

Because the room had no fireplace.

What is the best way to keep a Boy Scout uniform clean?

Don't put it on a scout.

How is a boy scout's broken leg like his mother's skein of yarn?

Neither can be used until it is knit.

Scoutmaster: "Why are you running?"

Scout: "I'm trying to keep a fight from starting, sir."

Scoutmaster: "Between whom?"

Scout: "Between me and the big guy from Troop 106, sir."

Why did the little scout have such a difficult time helping the little old lady across the street?

She didn't want to cross that street.

Why do all scouts put on their right shoe first?

It would be pretty stupid of them to put on the wrong one.

Why did the scout never hit his thumb with a hammer?

He always had a cub hold the nail.

The eagle scout had just received a new uniform mailed to him by his proud grandmother who was never very certain of sizes.

"How does it fit?" his parents wanted to know.

"Actually it isn't all that much too big," answered the scout from his bedroom. "Only the pants are a bit loose under my armpits."

What did the mother lion say to her cub when she caught him chasing a little scout around and around a tree?

"How many times must I tell you not to play with your food!"

What happened to the scout who missed the bus and was late getting home from the pack meeting?

He caught it at home.

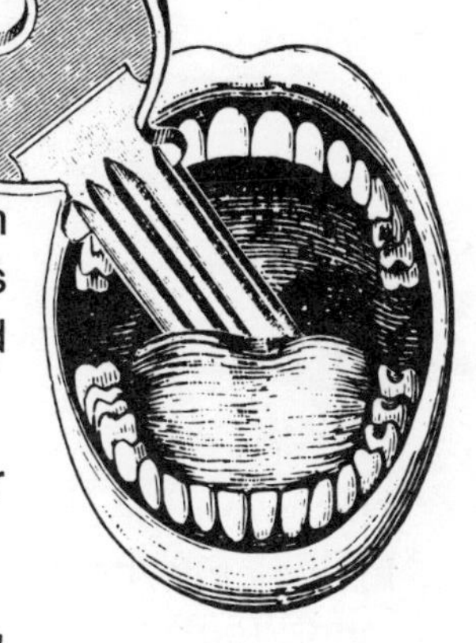

The scoutmaster had carefully gone through the required first-aid instruction. Now he was checking to be certain his boys understood the basic principles he had taught.

"Joe, what would you do if your baby brother swallowed your house key?" he asked.

Joe, after thinking a few seconds, answered, "I'd go in through my bedroom window."

What did the scout do when someone put his bugle in the freezer?

He played it cool.

Scoutmaster: "Joe, what steps should you take if you meet a bear in the forest?"

Joe: "Long ones, sir."

What must a scout do before getting out of his uniform?

Get into it.

Why was the scout so hard on his new uniform?

He wore it out in public the day he got it.

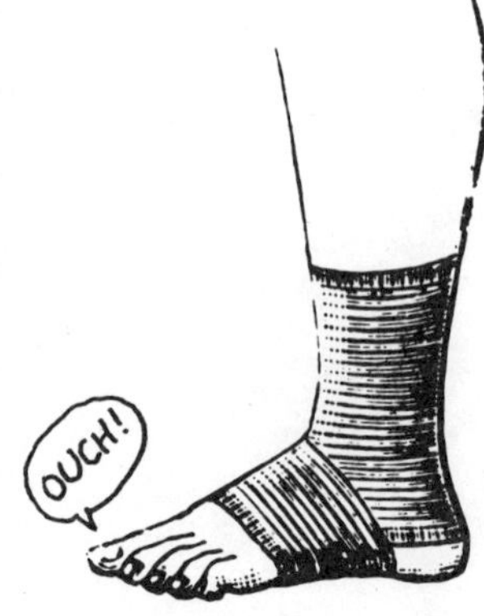

Scoutmaster: "All right, men. We've hiked eleven miles. Everyone who is too tired to hike another five miles take one pace forward."

Every scout except for Tenderfoot Tommy stepped forward.

Scoutmaster: "Is Tommy the only one of you with any courage?"

Tenderfoot Tommy: "Sir, I'm just too tired to take the one step forward."

The troop leader had taken about all the foolishness he could stand from a group of tenderfoot scouts out on their first hike. It was too much when a little scout sidled up to him and asked, "Do you know what has thirty legs, a large head, and is purple and red in alternating stripes?"

"No, I don't, nor do I care," snapped the short-tempered leader.

"Well," said the little scout, "it just dropped from a tree onto your neck and I thought you should know about it."

Where do scouts sleep when they are dog tired?

In pup tents.

Lincoln's Birthday

On February 12, 1866, less than a year after his death, Abraham Lincoln's birthday was first celebrated in Washington, D.C. In 1876 the first statue to his memory was erected in Washington. In 1892 Illinois became the first state to make his birthday a legal holiday. In 1909 over a million people in New York City attended special Lincoln Day ceremonies. In 1914, on his birthday, ground was broken for the Lincoln Memorial in Washington, D.C. It was completed in 1922 and is visited by millions of people each year. Despite these evidences of respect and love, Lincoln's birthday is not celebrated in a number of states today.

Abraham Lincoln was born on a Kentucky farm February 12, 1809. Two years later the family moved a few miles away to Knob Creek. When they could be spared from the farm chores, Abe and his sister Sarah went to a log schoolhouse.

When Abe was still a boy, the family moved to Indiana, where they bought a farm from the government. Abe and his father began to clear 160 acres of forest to make their farm. This was when Abe learned to use an ax, which he later wrote about as "that most useful instrument."

In 1818 his mother died. The next year Abe's father remarried and Abe's new mother brought her own children with her to join Abe and Sarah.

Though he spent only about one year in school, Abe worked at becoming educated. He walked miles to borrow books and read at night after working all day. He did math problems on a board that he shaved clean after it was filled so he could use it again.

By the time he was a teen-ager Abe stood six feet four inches tall. His hard work had made him extremely strong.

When he was nineteen he helped take a flatboat to New Orleans. In 1830 the family moved to Illinois. The following year Abe again floated a flatboat to New Orleans. After that trip he got a clerk's job in New Salem, Illinois.

In 1832 he served ninety days as a soldier in the Black Hawk War against the Indians. He didn't fight any Indians but said he had a lot of fights with mosquitoes.

That same year Abe ran for a state office and was defeated. He then started a store with a partner. They went broke, and when the partner died Abe had to pay all the debts of both himself and his partner. This honesty helped earn his nickname of "Honest Abe."

In 1834 he was elected to the Illinois legislature, where he served for eight years. Also in 1834 he began to study law by "reading" law. Three years later he became a lawyer. In 1842 he married Mary Todd. For several months he and his wife lived in a boarding house in Springfield where they paid four dollars a week in rent. Later they bought a small house where they lived when their children were born.

In 1846 Abe was elected to the United States House of Representatives. Two years later he returned to his law practice. In 1858, he ran against Stephen Douglas for the United States Senate. They debated the question of slavery before large groups of voters. Lincoln lost the election. Two years later, however, he was elected President. In that election he received more votes than did any of his three opponents, but fewer than the total cast for the others. Thus Lincoln was a minority President.

Shortly after his election the Civil War began. Lincoln is probably as well remembered for his Gettysburg Address on November 19, 1863, as for any other thing he did or said. In 1864 he was reelected President.

On April 9, 1865, the Civil War ended. Five days later Lincoln went to a play at Ford's Theatre in Washington, D.C. That Good Friday evening an actor, John Wilkes Booth, shot Lincoln while the President watched a play. The next morning Lincoln died. Upon his death a government official said, "Now he belongs to the ages."

The theater was closed following Lincoln's death and was not opened again until 1968. It is now a museum. In 1975 President Ford became the first President since the death of Lincoln to visit the theater.

The funeral train carrying Lincoln's body home took two weeks to travel to Springfield, Illinois. Crowds of mourners waited at each station for a chance to view the casket. Legend says that at midnight on the night of April 27 that funeral train still runs. Lincoln's black coffin may be clearly seen on the train, which is also draped in black. It is also said that on that day clocks are likely to run slow in their own tribute to a great American.

When is a piece of wood most like President Lincoln?

When it becomes a ruler.

Why was Abraham Lincoln buried at Springfield?

Because he was dead.

GOOD THINKING.

How did Lincoln's height compare to that of other men of his time?

They all stood over two feet.

Why did Lincoln sneeze four times?

He had a cold and couldn't help it.

Sarah: "If Abraham Lincoln were living today, people would say he was a remarkable man."

John: "They certainly would! He would be the world's oldest living man."

Why did Lincoln have to go to Washington, D.C., when he became President?

Because Washington would not come to him.

What did Lincoln keep even though he was a generous man?

His temper.

Teacher: "Johnny, how are Lincoln and Washington different?"

Johnny: "Lincoln once lived in Washington, but Washington never lived in Lincoln!"

Teacher: "Susie, what can you tell us about Lincoln's Gettysburg Address when he was President?"

Susie: "Gee, I thought he lived in Washington when he was President."

Isn't it amazing that so many famous people such as Abraham Lincoln were born on holidays!

Why is a bird on a fence like a Lincoln penny?

It has a head on one side and a tail on the other.

What did Abraham Lincoln become after he was forty-five?

Forty-six.

Did you know Lincoln was so tall that in the morning when he wanted to shave he had to stand on a ladder to reach his chin?

When Lincoln asked for a bed eight feet long, what did the innkeeper say?

"That's a lot of bunk."

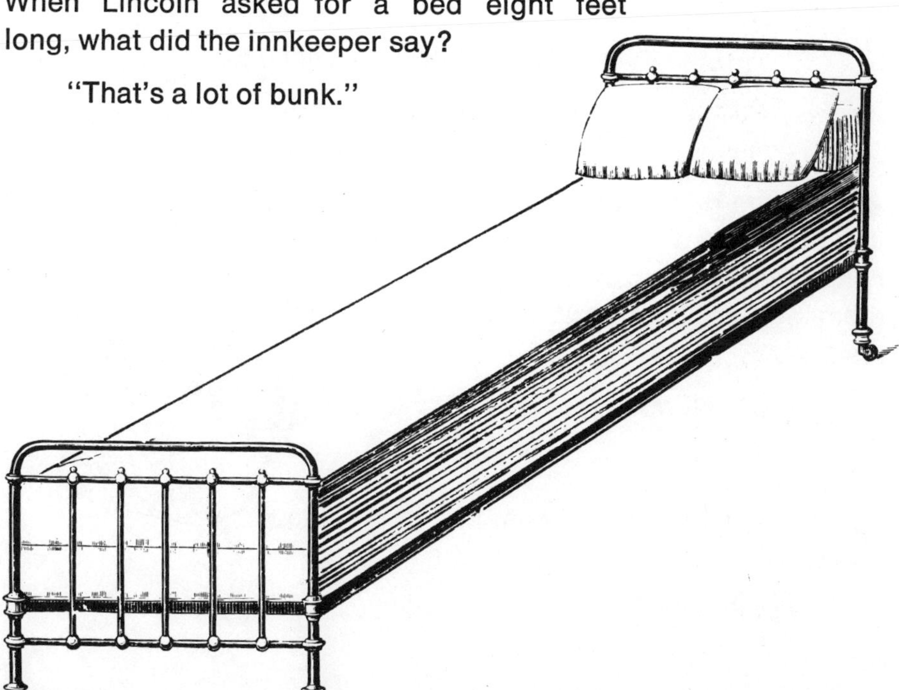

When Lincoln became President he was much like a book. Why?

Both Abe and the book had titles.

Abe Lincoln never had it and never wanted it, but if he had had it he wouldn't have given it up for the world. What was it?

A bald head.

When Lincoln was a young man, he worked in a general store and ran the butcher shop. At the time Abe was six feet four inches tall and wore size fourteen shoes. What did he weigh?

Meat, naturally.

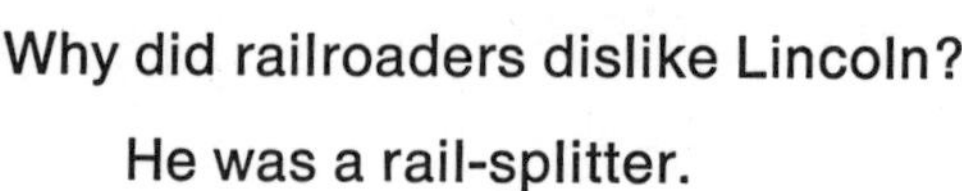

Why did railroaders dislike Lincoln?

He was a rail-splitter.

After a long day's work, Abe returned home to find the cabin dark. He entered his room carrying a match, a candle, and a lamp. In the room was a fireplace. Which should he light first?

The match would be his best bet.

When the family farm was producing, how was Abe unkind to the field of corn?

He pulled its ears.

Which question troubled Lincoln most during the time of the Civil War?

It wasn't any question that bothered him. It was the answers he had the trouble with.

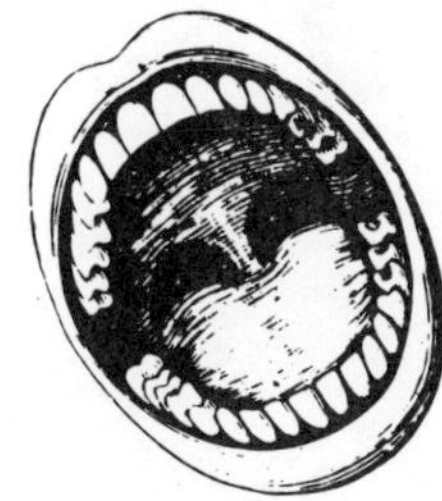

Why did Lincoln eat less than shorter men?

When he swallowed, a little went a long way.

As a boy, Lincoln did most of his studying by the light of the fireplace and by candlelight. Which type of candle did Abe find burned longer?

No candles burn longer. They all burn shorter.

When did Abe's hens become roosters?

Every night on the chicken roost.

St. Valentine's Day

Though Saint Valentine's Day has been celebrated since the Middle Ages, its origin is something of a mystery. First, there were several Saint Valentines. We know of at least three and there seem to have been as many as seven or eight. One of the early Valentines was thrown in jail for helping Christians. While in jail he was said to have cured the jailer's blind daughter, with whom he fell in love. His letters to her were signed "From your Valentine." Eventually poor Valentine was beheaded. Another Valentine performed marriages, which the emperor of Rome had forbidden. The emperor wanted no marriages or engagements so it would be easier to raise an army. That unfortunate Valentine was thrown into jail, where he died.

Just how the idea of people in love came to be associated with Saint Valentine's Day is a bit uncertain, even though at least two Valentines were in love or helped those who were.

Our best guess is that Valentine's Day goes back to a Roman festival called Lupercalia. When this festival was celebrated on February 15, girls put their names in huge urns or vases. Boys each drew a name from the urn. The girl and the boy who drew her name were considered sweethearts for the coming year. This custom was later popular in England. There the boy pinned the name of his sweetheart to his sleeve and wore it for several days.

Several times the Christian Church tried to stop or at least change the celebration of Saint Valentine's Day. The Church wanted the holiday to become a time of honoring saints. Each time this change was attempted it failed. Boys and girls were always more interested in one another than in learning about the saints.

As early as 1415 the first valentine love poems were written by a prisoner to his wife. By the mid 1600s the idea of sending valentine verses was common, at least in England. In the early 1700s booklets of valentine verses were being sold. One bought the booklet, found a verse, and copied it on a sheet of fancy paper. About 1800, printed valentines began to appear, and forty years later valentines with moving parts were being manufactured. In 1870 comic valentines could be purchased. Though these comic valentines were often in pretty poor taste, they were the ancestors of many of today's comic greetings.

A few superstitions have become a part of Saint Valentine's Day. Birds and animals are believed by many to begin mating on February 14. A girl will marry the first eligible man she sees on Valentine's Day. If you pin bay leaves to your pillow and eat a hard-boiled egg filled with salt, you will dream of your lover on Valentine's Eve. If an unmarried girl goes to the graveyard at midnight on Valentine's Eve, she will see a vision of the man who is to become her husband.

This celebration remains one of our most fun holidays. It does not really matter how many Saint Valentines actually lived. The fact that we enjoy celebrating Saint Valentine's Day is the important thing.

"If you can't guess who I am in three guesses, I'm going to kiss you."

She: "The Easter bunny, Santa Claus, Abe Lincoln?"

When Joe asked his girl to go steady on Valentine's Day, she insisted they walk a few blocks before she answered. Having walked the required distance, she said, "Yes, I'd love to go steady with you."

"Swell," Joe answered, "but why did we have to walk so far before you made up your mind?"

"I don't believe in love at first site," the lovely replied.

Missy: "Whose valentine are you going to be?"

Prissy: "Well, Joe is handsome, Pete is smart, and Fred is clever, but I think I'll be Bob's valentine."

Missy: "Why? What's so special about Bob?"

Prissy: "He has a wealthy father."

How can a girl keep a boy's love on Valentine's Day?

By not returning it.

When a boy breaks a date on Valentine's Day it means he has to.

When a girl breaks a date on Valentine's Day it means she had two.

When is a girl not a girl?

On Valentine's Day, when she is a dear.

"Knock, knock."
"Who's there?"
"Olive."
"Olive who?"
"Olive you."

One sweet thing to another: "What is the secret of your youth?"

Second sweet thing: "I lie about my age."

"My valentine has an hourglass figure," said Tom.

"Wow!" replied Dan.

"Unfortunately, time is running out," Tom lamented.

The young man had given the girl of his dreams an enormous valentine, but she remained cool to him.

"You can learn to love me," he pleaded.

"Perhaps," the sweet young thing said. "After all, I did learn to take cod liver oil and eat spinach."

Why did the lad take so long to write a Valentine's Day letter to his girl?

She was a slow reader.

Why did the valentine arrive wet in the mail?

It came postage dew.

What happened to the fellow who was knee-deep in love?

He got put on the lovely's wading list.

First girl: "I caught my boyfriend flirting."

Second girl: "Is there any other way?"

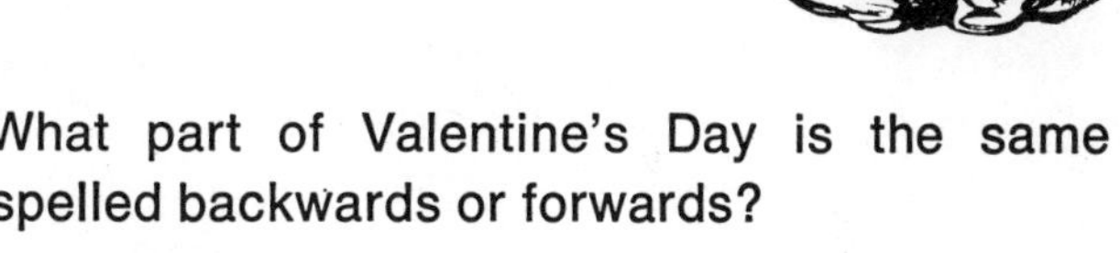

What part of Valentine's Day is the same spelled backwards or forwards?

Noon.

What does a valentine envelope say when you lick it?

It just shuts up and says nothing.

She: "Do you love me enough to die for me?"

He: "No, my love is more of an undying love."

Advice to pretty girls on Valentine's Day: Never let a kiss fool you or a fool kiss you.

Ardent boy to his girl on Valentine's Day: "May I hold your hand?"

Girl: "It isn't so heavy. I can hold it myself."

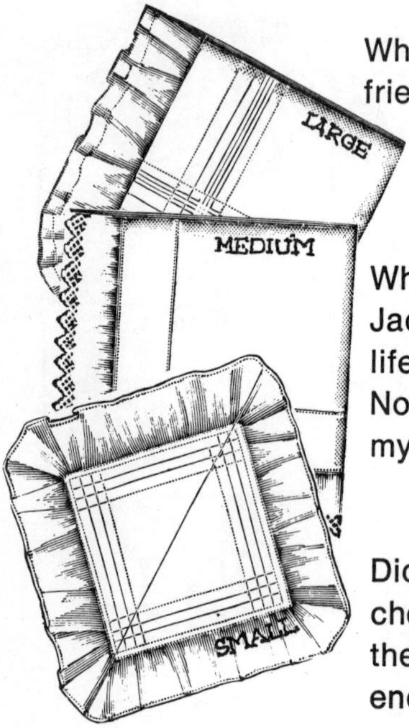

Why did Jake decide not to give his girl friend a handkerchief for Valentine's Day?

He forgot her nose size.

When Jill did not receive a valentine from Jack she sobbed, "He has ruined my whole life. My heart is broken for ever and ever. Not only that," she added, "but he has spoiled my whole day."

Did you hear about the love-struck lad who checked out *How to Hug* from the library and then found out it was a volume from a set of encyclopedias?

Joe: "Is it true opposites attract?"

Moe: "Must be. Why else would so many poor fellows marry rich wives!"

The young lad was preparing to mail a valentine to his girl friend. "May I put the stamp on myself?" he asked his mother.

"Of course," she replied, "but it might be better to put it on the envelope."

What is blue and square and arrives on February 14?

A valentine in disguise.

Boastful Bob to Timid Ted: "I told you I'd kiss Susan for Valentine's Day or die trying."

Timid Ted: "Well, did you do it?"

Boastful Bob: "When you read today's obituary column in the paper, my name won't be there!"

"Do you think I'm conceited?" she asked him shyly.

"Shucks, no," he replied. "Why do you ask?"

"Girls who are as beautiful as I am often are," she answered.

Washington's Birthday

"First in war, first in peace, and first in the hearts of his countrymen." These words perhaps best describe the only man whose birthday is a national holiday, George Washington. Thirty-two states have counties named Washington. Our national capital is also named for him.

George Washington was born in Virginia on February 22, 1732. He was actually born on February 11, according to the calendar then in use. When the calendar changed, so did his birthday. George's family moved to Mount Vernon when George was three. Four years later they moved to another farm, though Mount Vernon was still owned by the family. George later inherited Mount Vernon and lived there at the time of his own death.

George only went to school for seven or eight years. His

father died when George was eleven, and George helped run the plantation and manage the twenty slaves his family owned. When he was fourteen he wanted to join the British navy, but his mother stopped him. Two years later George learned to survey land and got a job surveying the five million acres owned by Lord Fairfax. George worked as a surveyor until 1752, and, with his earnings, managed to buy land for himself.

In 1753, he became a major in the Virginia militia. As a part of this job he became involved in the French and Indian War. Several times he came close to death. In 1755 he was an aide to General Braddock when Braddock's force was beaten by the French. Washington then spent the rest of that war commanding colonial troops.

In 1759 he married Martha Custis, who was a wealthy widow with two children. At the time he was a member of the Virginia legislature, a job he kept for sixteen years. In addition to learning about government he became a skillful farmer. When George inherited Mount Vernon he worked hard at making it a fine plantation.

When the colonies began having serious trouble with Britain, Washington was elected to the First Continental Congress in 1774. The next year he went to the Second Continental Congress, which chose him to be commander in chief of the colonial army. Washington did not want war and refused to take a salary for the job. When the Congress chose him, Washington said, "I do not think myself equal to the command I am honored with."

Though the Revolutionary War went badly for him much of the time, Washington finally led his ragged, hungry, and discouraged troops to victory. After the war ended, some people wanted Washington to become a king. He refused, saying Americans did not need a king.

In 1787 he was sent to the Constitutional Convention, which was writing the laws for the new nation. In 1788 he was elected the first President of the United States. As President he went to New York, since we had no national capital. Only eleven states were part of the nation at that time. Later, Congress made Philadelphia the capital rather than New York. Washington served two terms as President and refused a third term when it was offered to him.

As President, Washington set up a cabinet to help advise him on running the nation. He encouraged the United States not to become involved in European affairs and did all he could to keep us away from wars.

When Washington left office he retired to Mount Vernon. There he died on December 14, 1799. His last words were, " 'Tis well."

The first public celebration of Washington's birthday was by a group of soldiers at Valley Forge in 1778. In 1781 a group of French officers held a birthday dinner for him. The next year the citizens of Richmond, Virginia, celebrated his birthday, and in 1784 New York honored him on his birthday. In 1789 the Tammany Society decided to celebrate Washington's birthday from then on.

In 1791 a military parade was held on Washington's birthday in Philadelphia, which was still the capital. That same year, Washington laid out the boundaries for the new capital city, which was later named for him. Congress set February 22, 1800, as a day of national mourning following his death in 1799.

The cornerstone for the Washington Monument was laid July 3, 1848. However, the monument was not finished until 1885, because no work was done on it from 1854 until 1880. When it was finished, it stood 555½ feet high, a fitting memorial to a great man.

We have all heard stories about Washington's boyhood adventures. Unfortunately, many of them never happened. A man named Mason Locke Weems created many Washington stories. Weems told about Washington chopping down his father's cherry tree. He also told of Washington throwing a dollar across the Potomac. It was also Weems who invented the tale of the Indian who fired at Washington seventeen times without hurting him. In spite of such inventions, we honor George Washington as a man who loved his nation and served it well.

What famous American had the largest family?

George Washington. He was the Father of Our Country.

How did the student know that Washington was a soldier and not a sailor?

He saw a picture of Washington crossing the Delaware and knew any sailor would know better than to stand up in a rowboat.

What did Washington's father say to George when he brought home his report card?

"George, why did you go down in history?"

When was George a jump ahead of Martha?

When they played checkers.

Poor George was tired and cold when he finally stopped at a wayside inn. "Can you give me a room and a bath?" he asked the innkeeper.

"A room, yes," answered the other, "but you'll have to give yourself the bath, General."

Boy: "Why did George Washington chop down the cherry tree?"

Girl: "I don't know."

Boy: "Stumped you, didn't I?"

What bull did George shoot during the Revolution?

A bullet.

When was George's pet dog most likely to enter the house at Mount Vernon?

When George left the door open.

When Washington left the presidency, that office was like a decayed tooth. How so?

It required filling.

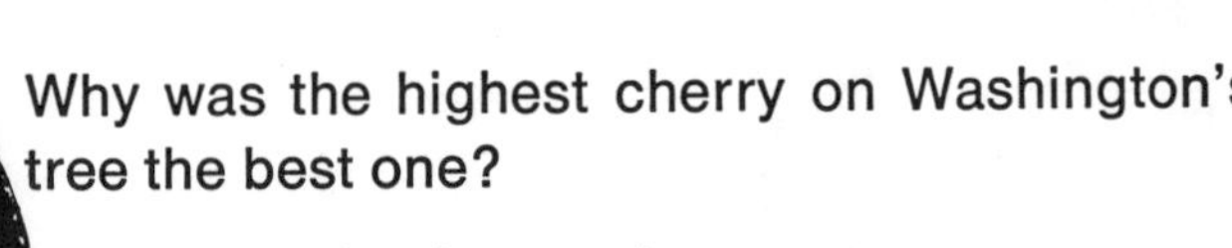

Why was the highest cherry on Washington's tree the best one?

It was the tip-top cherry.

Professor: "What great event occurred in 1732?"

Student: "George Washington was born."

Professor: "And what historic event took place in 1763?"

Student, after thinking a moment: "Washington had his thirty-first birthday."

When George was surveying the wilderness, an Indian shot an arrow at him but missed. How did George refer to this incident?

He said he had an arrow escape.

What did Washington and his men want to keep at Valley Forge?

Warm.

Why did George Washington refuse to play checkers?

He said no one should ever be crowned king in the United States.

What did George Washington's nephew say when Martha Washington boasted that her husband could do anything that needed doing on their plantation?

Why didn't George want Martha to learn a foreign language?

He said one tongue was enough for any woman.

Where did George Washington stand when he became our first President?

On his feet.

Why didn't George's father spank him for chopping down the cherry tree?

George was still holding the hatchet!

Why did the ladies like General Washington so much?

Every woman enjoys a good offer, sir.

Though he was a great general, what was the one thing Washington could never conquer?

Sleep.

As George grew older, what caused Martha to say his teeth were like stars?

They came out at night.

What should a pair of false teeth remind you of?

The George Washington Bridge.

What was Washington most famous for?

His memory. We built a monument to it.

When were Washington's men only partially complete?

When they were in quarters at Valley Forge.

One of George's Mount Vernon neighbors complained about everything. Nothing suited him. One spring day he stood talking to George about the bad weather.

"Why, we've had such bad weather I'd predict you won't get even a bushel of apples off that tree over there," he muttered.

"I daresay you're right," George agreed. "That is a cherry tree."

Once, during the Revolutionary War, General Washington went sleepless for nineteen days. How did he manage to carry on?

He slept nights.

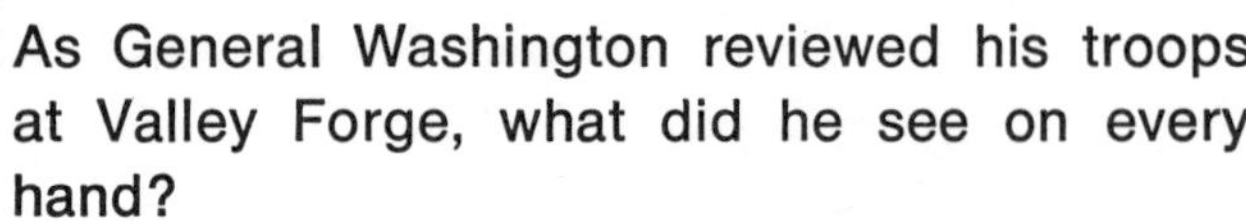

As General Washington reviewed his troops at Valley Forge, what did he see on every hand?

Gloves.

Why was American history easier for George Washington than it is for you?

He had a lot less American history to learn.

What did George Washington give but always keep?

His word.

When did General Washington's horse eat the most?

When there wasn't a bit in his mouth.

Why is a dog chasing a rabbit like George Washington without his wig?

A little hare goes a long way.

Girl Scout Day

An American, Mrs. Juliette Gordon Low, is given credit for founding the Girl Scout program. Mrs. Low was from Georgia, but spent a great deal of time in England because her husband was English. It was while she was living in London that Mrs. Low met Sir Robert Baden-Powell, who had started the Boy Scout program.

Mrs. Low also discovered that Baden-Powell's sister, Agnes, had started a program for girls. It was called the Girl Guides. Mrs. Low was very impressed with the idea. Later she talked about the program with her niece, Daisy Gordon. On March 12, 1912, Daisy and ten other girls met in Mrs. Low's stable in Savannah, Georgia. On that day the Girl Scout program had its beginning in the United States. It wasn't until 1915, however, that the name of the program became Girl Scouts.

Today over 3½ million girls and women take part in the Girl Scouts in the United States. The program is also carried on in more than ninety other nations of the world. Both the Girl Scout and Girl Guide programs still exist. Some nations have scouts, while others have guides.

Brownie Scouts are the youngest members of the scouting group. Then come Junior Girl Scouts, Cadette Girl Scouts, and finally Senior Girl Scouts. Just as with the Boy Scouts, the Girl Scouting program is designed to make healthy and happy citizens of its members.

Leader: How do you make an apple turn-over?"

Girl scout: "You might tickle it in the ribs."

What is purple and comes in a blue box?

A disguised girl scout cookie.

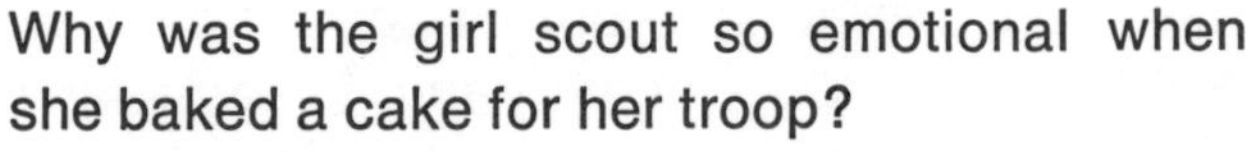

Why was the girl scout so emotional when she baked a cake for her troop?

It was a stirring experience.

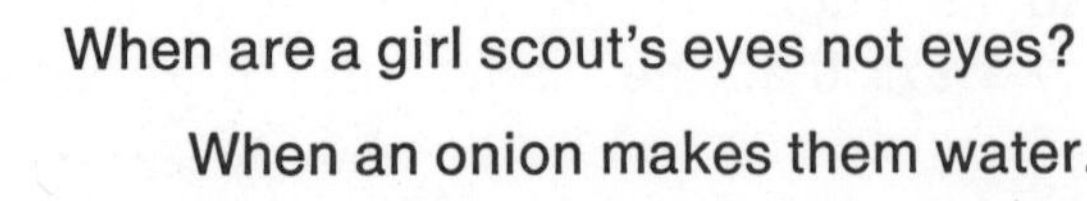

When are a girl scout's eyes not eyes?

When an onion makes them water.

Why shouldn't a boy scout try to court a girl scout in the garden?

Because the corn has ears and the potatoes have eyes.

Leader: "What should you do if a man-eating tiger chases you through the forest?"

Little girl scout: "I wouldn't do anything. I'm a girl."

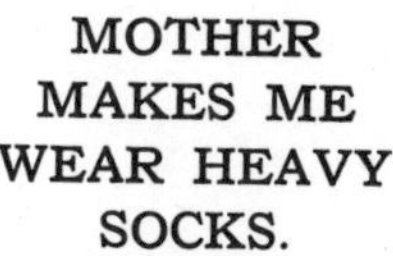

What did the girl scout say when her troop leader remarked that her shoes were on the wrong feet?

"These are the only feet I have."

Why did the girl scout cookie cry?

Its mother had been a wafer too long.

What did the chubby girl scout say to her friend after studying a weight and height chart?

"According to this chart, I am three and a half inches too short."

What is the last thing a girl scout removes before going to bed at night?

Her feet from the floor.

Why did the girl scout spend her day of community service putting on a wet coat?

She was painting.

What does a Girl Scout become after she is eleven years old?

Twelve years old.

When do girl scouts have four legs?

When there are two of them.

What does half a girl scout cookie resemble most?

The other half.

What word can a girl scout pronounce quicker by adding a syllable?

Quick.

What happened to the girl scout when she swallowed her spoon while working on her cooking merit badge?

She could not stir.

Why did the girl scout buy a new uniform?

Because she couldn't leave the store without paying for it.

Girl scout: "I didn't sell any cookies at the corner house. They had a dog that barked at me."

Leader: "Barking dogs don't bite."

Girl scout: "You and I know that, but what if the dog doesn't?"

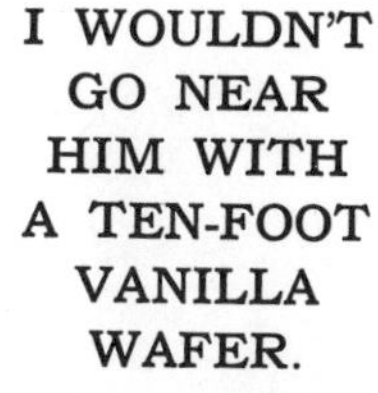

What is green, has eight legs, and sings?

A girl scout quartet.

How can you tell the girl scout from her twin?

He is a lot taller and his hair is a different color.

What does every girl scout in the world have?

A name.

Why do girl scouts sell cookies?

They would rather sell them than give them away.

If a girl scout counted twenty houses on her right going to her scout meeting and twenty on her left coming home, how many houses did she count?

Twenty.

What is always before a girl scout, yet she can't see it?

Her future.

With which hand does a proper girl scout stir her hot chocolate?

Proper girl scouts use a spoon.

The little girl scout was having a terrible time on her first cookout. Finally an older girl asked what was wrong.

"I've left something at home I need," the little scout said.

"And what is that?" the older girl wondered.

"My mother," admitted the little scout.

One girl scout was discussing another scout with her mother. "Agnes is just like a ship coming into harbor," she said.

"How is that?" her mother wondered.

"She is always around the boys [buoys]," replied the jealous girl scout.

What happened when the girl scout tried to sweep out her room?

She couldn't, so she swept out the dirt and dust instead.

What bow can't a girl scout tie or untie?

A rainbow.

Why are girl scouts taught never to swim on full stomachs?

It is better to swim in water.

What do girl scouts do when it rains?

They let it rain, just like anyone else.

What is green and moves from house to house?

A girl scout selling girl scout cookies.

Why was the lovestruck girl scout gazing at the moon?

There was a man in it.

St. Patrick's Day

Patrick, the patron saint of Ireland, whose memory is honored on March 17, was not born in Ireland. He seems to have been born in Scotland, or England, or Wales, or perhaps even in France. The only thing certain is that he was a Roman citizen. The date of his birth was sometime between 373 and 395, and he died between 461 and 493. March 17 is considered to be most likely the date of Saint Patrick's death, though some people insist it is the date of his birth and a few suggest it is neither the date of his birth nor that of his death. To completely confuse the matter, there is a possibility there may actually have been two Saint Patricks, though we don't like to consider this.

When he was sixteen years old, Patrick was captured by a band of roving Irishmen and taken to Ireland, where he lived for six years as a slave of the Druids. During these years he had dreams and visions he thought came from God. As the result of one such dream he escaped from slavery and fled to Britain by boat. After he reached his home, another dream told him he was one day to free Ireland.

Saint Patrick entered the priesthood and eventually did return to Ireland in 432 or 433. There he started churches, schools, and a college. During his years of working for the Church, he was often opposed by the pagan Druids. Several times he came close to being stoned to death by them for the things he preached. Finally Saint Patrick became so upset with these savage people he put a curse on them to force them to allow him to preach Christianity.

The shamrock is said to have become a symbol of Saint Patrick's Day because of his use of the leaf in his preaching. Saint Patrick is supposed to have used the shamrock leaves to stand for the Holy Trinity of Father, Son, and Holy Ghost. Because of this, the shamrock has always been thought of as an important part of Saint Patrick's Day.

Among the miracles said to have been performed by Saint Patrick, the best-known deals with his driving the snakes out of Ireland. According to legend, Saint Patrick used a loud drum and a sermon to free Ireland of snakes. One old, especially tough snake decided not to leave. Saint Patrick built a box and asked the snake to get into it. The snake refused, saying the box was too small. After considerable discussion, the snake decided to prove Saint Patrick wrong. When he coiled into the box, Saint Patrick shut the lid and threw the box and snake into the sea.

Saint Patrick is also supposed to have raised people from the dead, including his own father. He is credited as well with making fire out of snow and killing demons who wished to harm him. Much of his power was said to come from his staff, which was supposed to have been given him by Christ during a vision.

When Saint Patrick is honored in Ireland, the holiday lasts three days and is a religious time. It is also traditionally the day the stock are driven to pasture for the summer. Farmers also plant their potatoes on that day.

This is a far cry from the American celebration of Saint Patrick's Day. From its first American observance in Boston, in 1737, until now it has been a time of good spirits and happy drinking. This is strange in a way, because Saint Patrick is supposed to have been opposed to the use of alcohol.

Today the holiday is observed by all Americans and not just those of Irish ancestry. The "wearing of the green" is a part of the day, just as are parades in many large cities. The most noted Saint Patrick's Day parade is along New York City's Fifth Avenue in front of Saint Patrick's Cathedral.

As a final mystery of Saint Patrick's Day, no one seems to know for certain where the custom of pinching those not wearing green originated or why. It certainly has nothing to do with Ireland's good patron saint, or does it?

What are red-headed leprechauns called in Ireland?

Leprechauns.

Why shouldn't you wear a green shirt and red socks on Saint Patrick's Day?

Those are Christmas colors.

What are you likely to grow if you march in the Saint Patrick's Day parade?

Tired.

What did the leader of the Saint Patrick's Day parade exclaim when only one-fourth of the marchers showed up to march in the parade?

"It won't be long now!"

Why do leprechauns wear green hats when it rains on Saint Patrick's Day?

To keep their heads dry.

Why did Larry dye his shirt and trousers green before going to the Saint Patrick's Day parade?

He was dyeing to make a good impression.

Why are Saint Patrick's Day and April 15 related?

On Saint Patrick's Day you wear green, and on April 15 the government takes your green.

When did the Irish potato change its nationality?

When it was french-fried.

First Leprechaun: "I'm thinking I don't much like the looks of your wife today."

Second Leprechaun: "Nor do I, but at least I'm not always worried about someone wanting to take her away from me."

Why is lightning shocking to shamrocks?

It doesn't know how to conduct itself.

The old leprechaun was discussing the problems of aging with a younger member of his clan.

"Many things cause me difficulty. Forgetting things is the most bothersome of them all," he complained.

"How long have you been troubled by this?" the younger leprechaun wanted to know.

"Troubled by what?" returned the aged leprechaun.

When are jealous people acceptable on Saint Patrick's Day?

When they turn green with envy.

What would you call an eight-foot-tall leprechaun who carried a large club?

Sir!

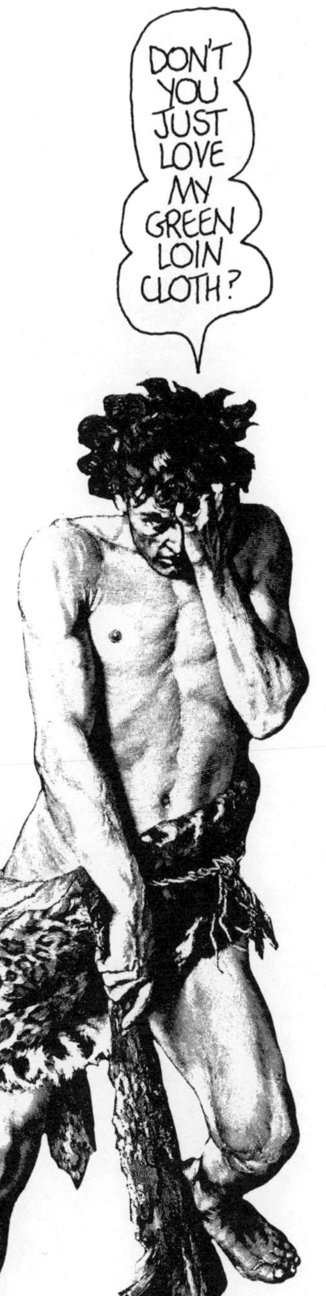

Why do so many people live in Ireland?

Its capital is constantly Dublin.

Why did everyone suddenly quit watching the Saint Patrick's Day parade?

The parade was over.

April Fool's Day

The really funny thing about April Fool's Day, or All Fool's Day, is that we don't know for sure just how the custom of fooling people began. Some say it is related to an old Roman festival that was celebrated on March 25. The day may have to do with the fact that the vernal equinox comes on March 21 and was a New Year for many people. Playing jokes may even be taken as a sign of joy at the end of winter and the coming of spring.

Most likely the custom is related to the fact that in 1582 the French made a great change in their calendar. This change moved New Year's Day from April 1 back to January 1, where it is now. Not everyone approved of the change, and some did not even know about it for quite some time. As a result, the first of April became a time of poking fun.

The French also noted that about the first of April a number of young fish began to appear in the streams. These foolish fish were not so wise and wary as their elders and were easier to catch. Thus April 1 became a time for the catching of the less wise and more foolish. Any person who was caught or tricked on April 1 was called an April fish. Perhaps the French children were the winners in all this. It became a custom to give the children a chocolate fish as an April Fool's Day present.

Sometime in the 1700s the English took up the habit of April-fooling one another. This had no connection with the French calendar change, because the English did not change their calendar until much later than did the French. For the English, April Fool's Day became known as a time for sending the less wise on fool's errands. Solemn Englishmen sent children on searches for hen's teeth and on other such impossible tasks. Today's pranksters delight in sending the unwary in search of left-handed wrenches and sky hooks.

The fool's errand, or the impossible search, seems to have long been a part of this special day. For hundreds and perhaps thousands of years the people of India celebrated the Feast of Huli on March 31, and unwary people found themselves going on ridiculous errands.

The Scots delighted in sending a letter by an unsuspecting messenger they called a gowk. Each person who got the letter read it, then sent the April gowk on down the road to another person. Of course, that was exactly what the letter said to do.

Naturally, when the European settlers came to the New World, they brought April Fool's Day with them. The variety of pranks played over the years is fantastic. Here are a few of the common and perhaps not so common April Fool's pranks of which we have heard.

The telephone has been a boon to pranksters. Thousands of people have been called and asked whether their refrigerator was running. When they said it was, they were told they had better stop it before it got away.

A somewhat more involved telephone prank requires several calls. The first caller asks, "Is Joe there?"

Naturally the one receiving the call suggests a wrong number.

A short while later another prankster calls and asks for Joe. Again he is told there is no Joe there. This continues for several calls, until finally the original prankster calls and says, "Hello, this is Joe. Have there been any calls for me?"

When plastic came into being, it helped April Fool's jokesters tremendously. One of the better of the plastic April Fool's jokes requires the prankster to put a plastic bag into his coat pocket. He then goes to a shop and orders a soft drink or a malt. When it is served he makes a great show of looking at his watch and exclaiming he is out of time. "I guess I'll have to drink this later," he says loudly. Then the joker stands up and pours the drink into his coat pocket while everyone looks on in disbelief.

We think the idea of putting a brick under a hat or can came from England. It is hard to resist kicking an old hat or a can lying in the street. Of course, a healthy kick that connects with a hidden brick can just about ruin one's April Fool's Day.

We know our last April Fool's trick did come from England. A fellow with a ball of string stops a passerby on the street and asks him to hold the end of the string if he would. "I've got to measure these shops and my helper took sick," is the way it goes. Once a sucker is caught, the prankster quickly unrolls the string and disappears around a corner. There he finds another sucker and gives him the ball of string to hold. At this point the joker ducks into a shop, leaving the two April fools holding the opposite ends of the string.

So much for April Fool's Day. From the jokes and riddles which follow, you can easily tell we are pretty April foolish ourselves.

Why did the little April fool stand on a ladder when he practiced his trumpet?

He wanted to be sure he could hit the high notes.

Little April fool: "April 1 was my very best day."

Friend: "How so?"

Little April fool: "Everyone said I was a perfect fool all day long."

Why did the little April fool take a sack of oats to bed with him?

To feed his nightmares.

What did the little April fool call a tangerine?

A loose-leaf orange.

Why did the little April fool get angry with her alarm clock?

It was always going off when she was asleep.

What did the little April fool's father say after looking at his son's terrible report card?

"With grades like these, at least I know you aren't cheating."

How did the little April fool raise corned beef and cabbage?

With his fork.

What did the little April fool do when he dropped a slice of limburger cheese in the toaster?

Got out of the kitchen as quickly as possible.

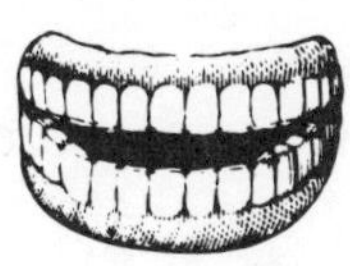

What did the little April fool say when her mother said, "Be sure to use plenty of toothpaste when you brush."

"That's all right, none of my teeth are loose."

Why did the little April fool need a piece of scratch paper?

His pen was itching.

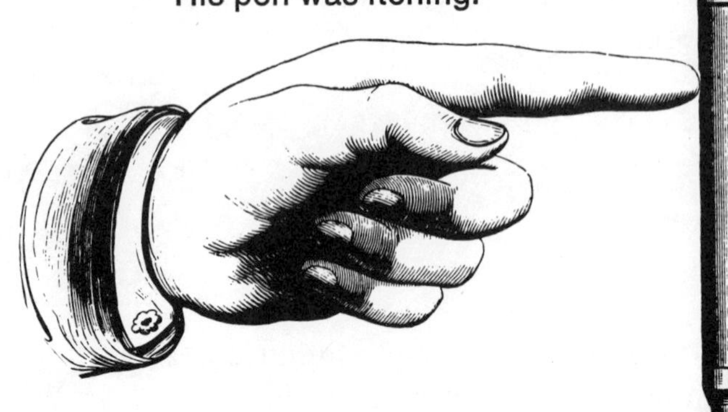

Teacher to little April fool: "Will you use a ruler to draw a straight line?"

Little April fool: "Wouldn't it be better if I used a pencil?"

Why did the little April fool wish he had two sisters?

Because he had six sisters.

Why did the little April fool sleep on the chandelier?

She was a light sleeper.

Why did the little April fool throw her watch across the room?

She wanted to see time fly.

What did the little April fool do when he thought he was dying?

He went into the living room.

Why wasn't the little April fool's nose twelve inches long?

Because then it would have been a foot.

Why did the little April fool lose his job as elevator operator?

He couldn't learn the route.

Why did the little April fool climb onto the roof of his house?

He heard the drinks were on the house.

Why did the little April fool fill her shoes with dirt?

To help make her corns grow.

What did the little April fool say when he got pepper up his nose?

"This stuff is nothing to be sneezed at."

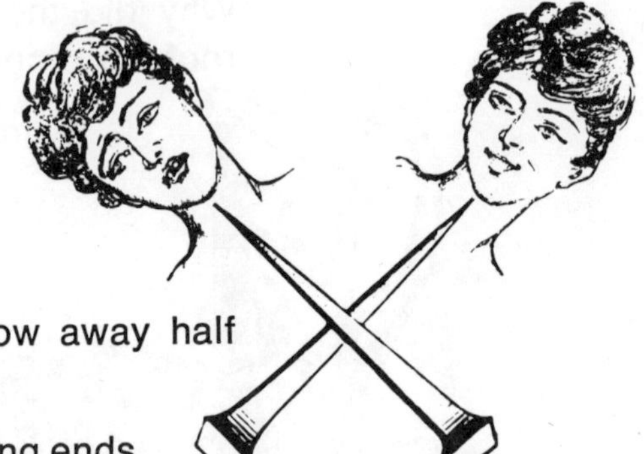

Why did the little April fool throw away half a sack of new nails?

Their heads were on the wrong ends.

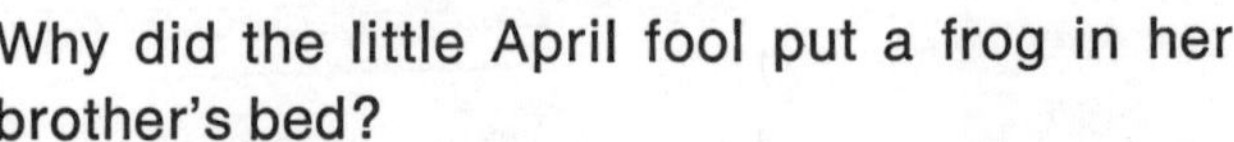

Why did the little April fool put a frog in her brother's bed?

She couldn't catch a snake.

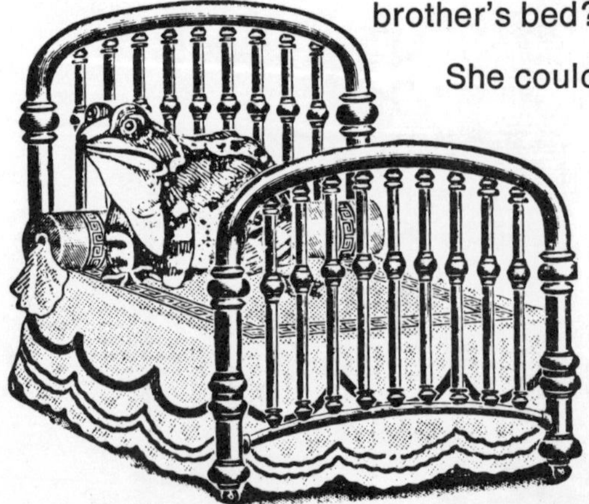

Why did the little April fool tell jokes to his father's car?

He wanted to see if it would crack up.

Why did the little April fool take sugar and cream to the movies?

She heard they had a new serial.

Little April fool: "Dad, this match won't light."

Dad: "What is the matter with it?"

Little April fool: "I don't know. It worked all right a minute ago."

Why did the little April fool stand behind the mule?

She thought she might get a kick out of it.

Why did the little April fool take a hammer to bed with him?

So he could hit the hay.

Later in the day his mother asked little April fool to help her with a broken window.

"This is real bad," little April fool confessed. "It is broken on both sides."

Why did little April fool go into the street with her bread and butter?

She was looking for some traffic jam.

Why did the little April fool rush to the store and buy a dozen loaves of bread?

He saw a sign saying "Raisin bread to-morrow."

Who gave the little April fool his black eye?

No one gave it to him. He fought for it.

How did the little April fool best like school?

Closed.

Friend: "Is it true your little brother talks to himself when he is alone?"

Little April fool: "I'm not sure. I've never been with him when he was alone."

Why did the little April fool stand before the mirror with his eyes shut?

He wanted to see how he looked when he was asleep.

Why did the little April fool eat a firecracker?

She wanted her hair to grow in bangs.

Teacher: "Name five things that contain milk."

Little April fool: "Ice cream, cheese, and three cows."

Easter

Easter is one of the two major Christian religious holidays. The other is, of course, Christmas. In the year 325 the Council of Nicaea decided to celebrate Easter on the Sunday following the first full moon after the vernal equinox. As an aid to setting this date, March 21 was decided to be the vernal, or spring, equinox. Thus Easter can come as early as March 22 or as late as April 25.

The word *Easter* itself probably came from the name of the Anglo-Saxon goddess of spring, Eostre. Of course, it is possible the name *Easter* may have come from the word *east,* which is the direction in which the sun rises.

This special day of religious celebration is observed in Christian churches the world over. However, as with many religious holidays, a number of customs have developed over the years that add further dimensions to the holiday.

Perhaps the best known of these customs have to do with the Easter rabbit and Easter eggs. Both were symbols of the spring goddess Eostre. For many people of many nations the egg has long been a symbol of life. It was the German settlers in Pennsylvania who brought the idea of the Easter rabbit and eggs to North America from Europe. Their children built nests for the Easter rabbit and were told that, if they were good children, the rabbit would lay Easter eggs in these nests.

An interesting set of beliefs has grown up concerning the Easter egg. Eggs were colored and eaten during spring festivals as far back as the time of ancient Egypt. The Persians gave eggs as presents at the time of the vernal equinox. Later on, the Greeks and Romans continued to dye and eat eggs.

The custom of dyed eggs came to Western Europe in the 1400s. Our best guess is that knights brought the idea home from the Crusades. Red was a popular color for these early Easter eggs. The color was said to stand for the blood of Christ. As the art of dying eggs progressed, religious symbols were often placed on eggs, and many colors were used on one egg.

Several kinds of Easter egg games developed over the years. One popular game involved rolling hard-boiled eggs at each other until only one egg was left unbroken. Another contest involved rolling as many eggs as possible down a hill without breaking them.

President Madison started the custom of rolling eggs on the Capitol lawn. Later, President Hayes moved the contest to the White House lawn because of complaints that the children were hurting the lawn in front of the Capitol. Many times the activity has been stopped, but in 1953 President Eisenhower again invited children to roll eggs on the White House lawn. Of course, the best-loved of all Easter egg games is that of hunting for eggs on Easter morning.

A custom that is far more popular with some than egg-rolling is that of wearing new clothing on Easter. Perhaps this dates from the time New Year's was celebrated in March and new clothing may have stood for a new beginning. Also, since the earth was putting on new clothing in spring, people felt they should do the same. The desire to show off fine new clothing resulted in Easter parades. The most famous of these parades was begun in the 1800s in New York City.

A number of superstitions have grown up around Easter. If you don't eat eggs on Easter, you will be bitten by a snake within the next year. If you have rheumatism and take a bath in a stream before sunrise on Easter morning, the condition will improve. If an egg laid on Good Friday is kept for a hundred years, its yolk will become a diamond. On Easter morning the sun dances. If you find two yolks in an Easter egg, you will gain money in the future. If it rains on Easter, there will be rain on the next seven Sundays.

Several foods other than eggs are also associated with the Easter festival. Ham has long been considered an Easter food. So have hot cross buns. If hot cross buns are eaten on Good Friday, your house will not catch fire during the coming year. If they are saved, they can keep you from having a bad accident. Should you become ill, an old hot cross bun is good medicine.

Though many Easter customs have nothing to do with Christ, they do not detract from the fact that Easter is a holiday with great significance to the world's Christians. As is true with many of our holidays, the basic reason for the holiday remains no matter how many additional customs develop through years of celebration.

The little girl opened her refrigerator Easter morning and discovered the Easter bunny sitting inside.

"What are you doing in there?" she asked.

"This is a Westinghouse, isn't it?" the Easter bunny asked.

"Yes, it is," the girl replied.

"Well," said the Easter bunny, "I'm just westing."

Why is a new Easter outfit like a large salad?

Both require a lot of dressing.

When does it rain Easter eggs?

When there is a change in the weather.

How is a happy golfer like an unhappy child with a broken Easter egg?

Both just made a hole in one.

What is the best year for the Easter bunny?

Leap year.

Little brother to big sister: "If you had ten Easter eggs and I asked you for five of them, how many would you have left?"

Big sister: "Ten."

Is it really true that carrots are good for the eyes?

Well, the Easter bunny doesn't wear glasses.

Where do Easter bunnies go for new tails?

To a retail store.

What did the grumpy man say to the Easter bunny?

"I don't care who you are, fuzzy tail, stop littering my lawn with those silly colored eggs!"

Shopper to clerk: "I'd like to try on that Easter outfit in the window."

Clerk: "Suit yourself, but I'd suggest you use the dressing room instead."

What would you have if you crossed an insect with an Easter bunny?

Bugs Bunny.

How is the ringing of church bells on Easter like a banana?

You can't enjoy either until they are pealed.

When will an Easter egg stop rolling downhill?

When it gets to the bottom of the hill.

How would you find the Easter bunny if he became lost?

Make a noise like a carrot and he will find you.

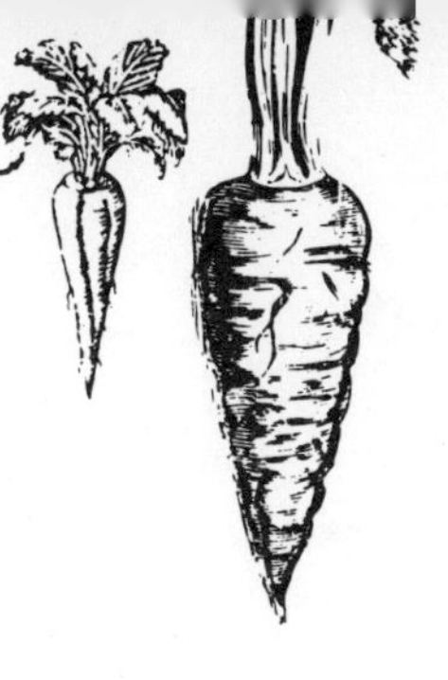

What is the best way for the Easter bunny to raise carrots?

Grab hold and pull.

What did the chick say when he saw the orange Easter egg?

"Look at the orange marmalade [Mama laid]."

When do Easter bunnies eat with their tails?

All the time; their tails never come off.

How can you eat an Easter egg without breaking its shell?

Have your mother break it for you.

Does the Easter bunny need a license?

Of course not. He is too young to drive.

Are hard-boiled Easter eggs healthy?

Did you ever hear one complain of poor health?

"And what did you give up for Lent?" one fellow asked of another.

"A hundred and sixty bucks for my wife's Easter outfit," was the quick reply.

Why did the Easter bunny hate to have weeds in his carrot garden?

If he gave them an inch, they would take his yard.

How does the Easter bunny get hens to lay hard-boiled eggs for him?

By giving them hot water to drink.

"There is a hair in my milk," cried little Johnny on Easter morning.

"So that's where the Easter bunny is hiding," his little sister cried.

If the Easter bunny never went out of the house, what would he be?

An ingrown hare.

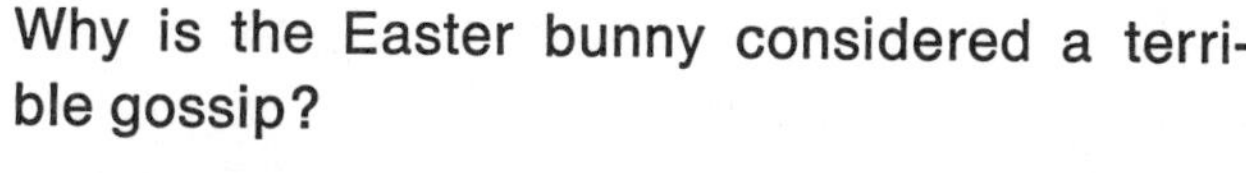

Why is the Easter bunny considered a terrible gossip?

No matter where he goes, he carries a tail with him.

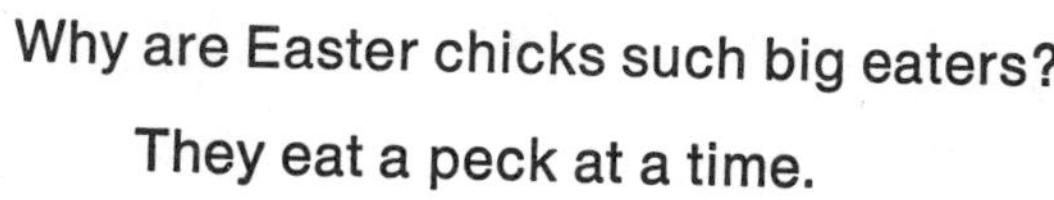

Why are Easter chicks such big eaters?

They eat a peck at a time.

"Some hens lay colored eggs," the Easter bunny told the young lad in the park.

"So what's so great about that?" the lad demanded.

"Can you do it?" asked the Easter bunny.

When the Easter bunny raided the old hen's nest for Easter eggs, how did she speak to him?

In fowl language.

Arbor Day

The idea of planting trees is an old one. The Aztec Indians were planting a tree to celebrate the birth of a child long before Columbus crossed the Atlantic. Indians in some parts of Mexico keep this custom alive by planting a tree at the time of the first full moon after a child is born. Years ago the people in some parts of Germany planted trees forty days after Easter.

The idea of Arbor Day began in Nebraska. When J. Sterling Morton moved to Nebraska he found open, wind-swept plains. He realized that trees planted as windbreaks would improve the quality of life for the people living there. He also suggested planting trees to honor people and to celebrate special occasions. After writing and speaking about the idea of Arbor Day, Mr. Morton finally spoke to the Nebraska State Board of Agriculture and Arbor Day began. The name *Arbor* he took from the Latin word meaning "tree." April 10, 1872, was Nebraska's first Arbor Day. On that one day over a million trees were planted.

The idea caught on rapidly. In 1885 Nebraska declared Arbor Day to be a legal holiday. Its celebration was to be on April 22, which was Morton's birthday. By 1887 the idea had spread to Britain, and from there to many nations of the world.

In Ballarat, Australia, for example, several thousand trees were planted as living memorials to dead soldiers. Each tree was dedicated to a soldier who had died for his country. In addition to nations, many famous people have believed in the idea of tree planting. Luther Burbank, the great "plant wizard," once said, "Do not build me a monument—plant a tree."

Today nearly all our states celebrate Arbor Day, though in most states it is not a legal holiday. Nor is it celebrated on the same day in all states. Some states combine Arbor Day with Bird Day, which is a logical combination of holidays. One or two states have two Arbor Days, one in the spring and one in the fall. This way trees may be planted at the time of year that best suits each kind of tree.

Since Arbor Day began in 1872, the number of trees planted has reached into the billions. Though this is not one of our major holidays, it may well be the most important to our environment and its ecology.

Why do trees planted on Arbor Day grow so tall?

What else has a tree got to do?

What did the beaver say to the tree?

It has been nice gnawing you.

What is the name of a cheese that grows on a tree?

A limburger.

How did the botanist identify the dogwood?

By its bark.

Which tree is named after an expensive coat?

The fir.

Which tree can be burned in the fireplace, yet still be itself?

The ash.

If you had a walnut tree with twelve branches and each branch produced ten acorns, how many acorns would you have in all?

None. Acorns don't grow on walnut trees.

Why was the tree petrified on Arbor Day?

A strong wind made it rock.

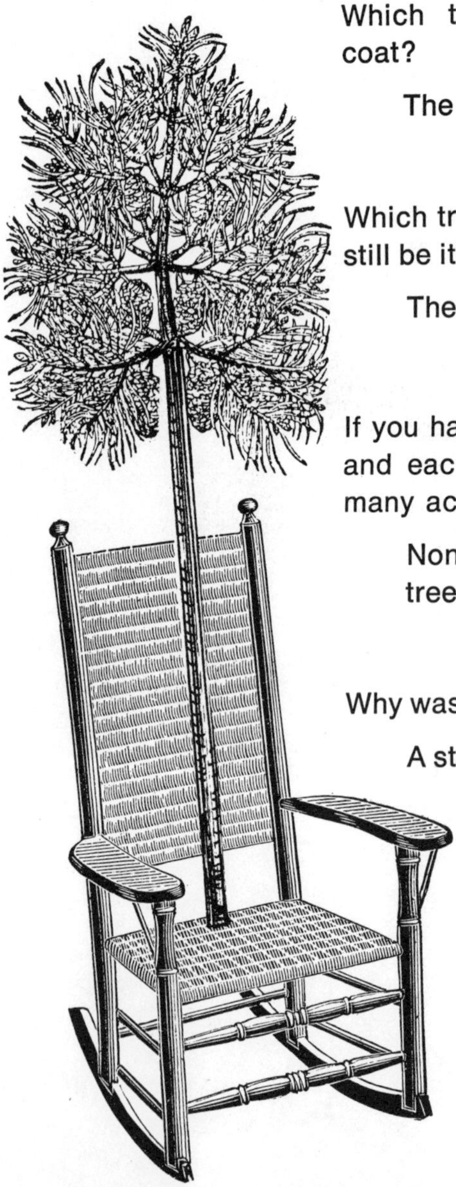

What is the difference between a funny Dutchman and a hollow tree?

One is a silly Hollander and the other is a hollow cylinder.

Which tree do carpenters use most often?

The plum.

Where would be the best place to deposit money that grew on trees?

In a branch bank.

Why are trees so silly?

They take off their clothing in winter and put it on in summer.

"What are you doing in my apple tree?" the irate farmer demanded.

"One of your apples fell off and I am trying to put it back on," the girl replied quickly.

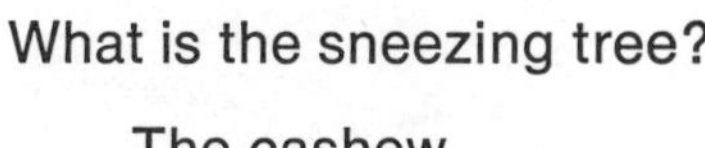

What is the sneezing tree?

The cashew.

Which tree is most closely related to a grasshopper?

The locust.

Why is the heart of a tree like the tip of a dog's tail?

It is the greatest distance from the bark.

Which is the most unhappy of all trees?

The weeping willow.

What is the most common tree found around the house?

The shoe tree.

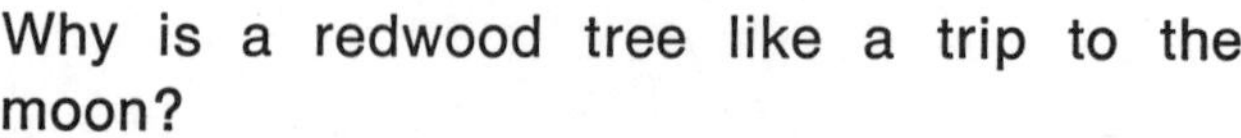

Why is a redwood tree like a trip to the moon?

Both have a long root (route).

Which tree is the sheep's closest relative?

The yew.

May Day

May Day is one of our very old holidays. It was celebrated by the Romans as early as 238 B.C. At that time it was a six-day celebration called Floralia honoring Flora, the goddess of flowers. The celebration began on April 28 and lasted until May 3. As one part of the celebration, Roman men carried flowering branches to the homes of the girls they loved. Even the Roman slaves liked the celebration because they got a day off from work.

When the Romans conquered the British Isles, the celebration of May Day went with them. The Druids there celebrated May 1 as a time of dividing the year in two. As a part of their celebration they built a new fire. Their fire was a part of their worship of the sun and may even have been used for human sacrifices. These ancient people also believed that if a man and his sweetheart ran through the smoke of a new fire it would bring them good luck for the coming year.

By the 1500s May Day was popular throughout England and in much of Europe. Bonfires were common as the people of Europe welcomed the coming of summer after a long winter. In England the hawthorn tree was used to make wreaths and garlands, which were used as May Day decorations. It was believed that if a woman got up early on May Day and washed her face in the dew, this would help keep her beautiful and her complexion clear.

By the Middle Ages every village in England had its own maypole. It became a contest to see which village could have the tallest maypole. In 1661 one of the tallest maypoles was brought to London from Scotland. It was carried in two pieces and put in place by a dozen sailors. Once it was up, it was 134 feet high.

It became common to have races and contests on May Day. The English chimney sweeps took May Day for their special day and held their own parade. In Sweden a play battle was held between men representing winter and those taking the part of summer. Of course, summer always won. After the battle a feast ended the celebration.

In 1886 the American Federation of Labor decided that May Day was a good time to begin the eight-hour working day. Their decisions led to strikes and riots and caused the death of a number of people. For a time May 1 became a European Labor Day as well. Since the 1920s Russia and other Communist nations have chosen May Day as a time for a great military parade in which they show off their weapons of war.

May Day has changed since it began, but still keeps a lot of the old ideas. In the United States we still have maypoles and May dances, and many places choose a Queen of May to reign over the celebration. May baskets are filled with candy or flowers and hung on the doors of friends. At Wellesley College the senior girls hold a hoop-rolling contest. The winner of the contest is supposed to be the first one of the group to marry.

On the evening before May Day the young men in parts of Switzerland decorate small pine trees, which they place on the doorsteps of their sweethearts. Attractive girls may end up with several pine trees, while their less beautiful friends may be left out entirely.

The lily-of-the-valley is the May Day flower in France. It is said that if someone you love gives you a bouquet of these flowers to wear, you may make a wish, which will come true so long as you are wearing the bouquet.

Since May Day is connected with romance, it is only natural that some interesting superstitions have come to be. It is said that when a girl first wakes up on May Day morning she should look at her mirror at an angle. If she does, she may catch a glimpse of the initials of the man she is to marry. At noon an unmarried girl can take a mirror and use it to cast a reflection in a well. It will form her lover's face on the water. However, if no lover's face appears, it means the poor girl will never marry but will become an old maid. Once in a while an unfortunate girl will see the reflection of a coffin instead of a handsome young man. This tells her she will not live to see the next year's May Day, which is a poor way indeed to celebrate this ancient day of fun and frolic.

What time is it when your pet Saint Bernard steps on your May basket?

Time to make a new May basket.

What did the girl say when she got only a vegetable in her May basket?

"That beets everything!"

The young fellow called his girl on the phone. "Would it be fair for you to get mad at me over something I didn't do?" he asked.

"Of course not, honey," the lass replied sweetly.

"Wow, that's a load off my mind," her guy answered, "because I didn't fix you a May basket."

How many pieces of candy does it take to fill a May basket?

One, if the piece of candy is big enough.

What happened when the little guy stubbed his toe while out delivering his May baskets?

One of his girl friends called a tow truck for him.

What is as big as the biggest May basket but doesn't weigh even an ounce?

The May basket's shadow.

Little Johnny fixed May baskets for all his girl friends. As the baskets sat on the table, Johnny saw a May basket between two baskets, a May basket behind two baskets, and a May basket in front of two baskets. How many girl friends did Johnny have?

Three.

Why should you keep your eyes open on May Day?

So you don't bump into something when you are out delivering May baskets.

"You would be a wonderful maypole dancer except for two things," she said to him.

"What two things?" he wondered.

"Your feet," she replied.

Mother's Day

Though festivals honoring mother goddesses date back to the time of the ancient Romans, Mother's Day is a relatively new holiday. The first Mother's Day was celebrated in Grafton, West Virginia, on May 10, 1908. That celebration was actually not in honor of all mothers but was intended to honor the memory of one mother. That was the mother of Miss Anna Jarvis, the woman who had the idea of our Mother's Day.

In 1907 Miss Jarvis began talking about a day to honor mothers. She wrote about her idea to congressmen, ministers, and others she thought might help her. Miss Jarvis's idea had rapid acceptance. Both West Virginia and Oklahoma had official Mother's Day celebrations in 1910. By the next year every state in the nation was celebrating Mother's Day. The next year a Mother's Day International Association was begun, and the holiday spread quickly to many nations of the world. In 1914

President Wilson asked that Mother's Day be observed as a national holiday.

An early kind of Mother's Day was common in England long before Miss Jarvis began our holiday as we now celebrate it. This English holiday was called Mothering Sunday or Mid-Lent Sunday. On that day, youths who had left home to work tried to return to visit their mothers. This was called Going A-Mothering. The children brought with them a small gift and a "mothering" cake as a present. Then, as now, it was common for the children in the family to do the household chores so their mother could attend church.

The English Mothering Sunday was celebrated from the early 1600s until the later 1800s. Gradually it died out, but when our Mother's Day began, the English once more celebrated the day honoring mothers in the nation. Yugoslavia, as well, celebrated a day honoring their mothers long before the beginning of Mother's Day in America. This special day was shortly before Christmas, however.

Since the beginning of Mother's Day, the carnation has been thought of as the special Mother's Day flower. This was because the carnation was the favorite flower of Mrs. Jarvis. At first only white carnations were used. After a time, though, the white carnation became the symbol of one whose mother was no longer living. Red carnations indicated that the mother of the wearer was still alive.

In 1934 the United States Post Office issued a special postage stamp commemorating Mother's Day. It had on it a copy of the famous painting of Whistler's Mother. After all, what could be more in keeping with the holiday than this famous painting!

Each year on the second Sunday in May we honor our mothers with their special day. Flowers and gifts and family gatherings are as appropriate now as they were in England hundreds of years ago.

What is the best way to remember Mother's Day?

Forget it just once!

Why didn't Dad speak to Mom all day?

He didn't want to interrupt what she was saying.

Long-suffering Mother wanted badly to be taken out for dinner and dancing on Mother's Day. "But I know better than to hope for it," she told a friend. "The only thing my husband takes out at night anymore is his teeth."

Why did Mrs. Smith say her husband was a man of rare gifts?

The last time he gave her a Mother's Day gift was eight years ago.

Why didn't Mother want to eat up the street on Mother's Day?

She hated the taste of concrete.

What do all mothers have in common?

They were once someone's daughters.

YAK, YAK
YAKKITY
YAK, YAK
YAKKITY
YAK,
YAK.

Why does Mom laugh at Dad's jokes?

Not because the jokes are clever but because Mom is.

Any man who thinks he is more intelligent than his wife is married to a smart woman!

If your uncle's sister isn't your aunt, who is she?

Your mother.

Why should we feel sorry for mother sheep?

Because they get fleeced so often.

Evelyn was explaining her mother's philosophy to a girl friend. "Every time Mom is down in the dumps, she gets a new hat."

Her friend's face brightened with understanding. "So that is where she gets them!"

What did the angry mother say as she spanked her naughty son who had just broken her Mother's Day present?

"I believe in getting to the bottom of things."

What word do mothers want when scolding naughty children?

The last one.

Children's Day

Children's Day is one of our holidays that is celebrated almost only by Protestant churches. There aren't any special department store sales or advertising promotions to accompany the day. And, outside the churches, the day usually passes without much notice.

The idea for Children's Day goes back many years to churches in Europe. There children were confirmed—formally admitted as responsible adults—in their church on May Day. In the procession the children always carried armloads of flowers. Since it was easier to find flowers in June than in May, the time for the celebration gradually changed.

When Children's Day was first observed in the United States in 1856, in Chelsea, Massachusetts, it was called Rose Sunday. Local churches held services that were of special interest to children. Later the Chelsea churches changed the day from Rose Sunday to Flower Sunday. Eventually it became known as Children's Day.

In 1868 the Methodist Church made Children's Day a formal church celebration. In 1883 the Presbyterian Church set the second Sunday in June as its Children's Day. Gradually other churches accepted the idea and now use the day for special children's services and programs.

Many churches also use this day as a time to honor the youths in their congregation who have graduated from high school or college. Some churches take up special offerings on Children's Day and use the money collected to provide college scholarships for members of the church who need help in completing their education.

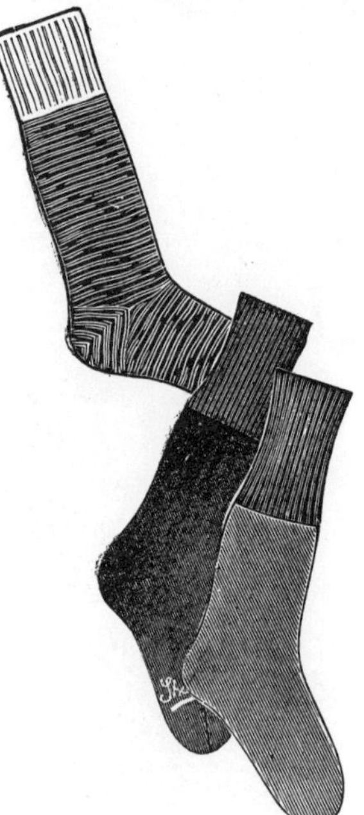

Why did the lad's grandmother send him three socks as a Children's Day present?

He had written that he had grown a foot since the last time she saw him.

Why was it lucky the young boy's parents named him Johnny?

Because that is what everybody called him.

Why did the baby's hair turn white?

His nearsighted mother kept powdering the wrong end.

What makes a child smart?

A spanking.

What do children make yet cannot see?

Noise.

The young mother purchased a box of diapers. The clerk added eight cents in tax. Why did she object to this?

She planned to use pins instead.

WELL, AT LEAST IT HAS A POINT!

THAT'S A TACKY JOKE.

Why did the girl cry when she lost her glasses?

She couldn't see how to find them.

When is a child not a child?

When it has a cold and becomes a little horse.

A wise old saying—the best way to handle a naughty child is to get to the bottom of things right away.

Another wise old saying—When a child does something clever, her parents speak of heredity. When she does something less than bright, her parents talk about the bad influence of friends and community.

What does a child in Algeria become after he is six years old?

Seven years old.

How did the boy know it wasn't dinnertime yet?

Because his mother told him to be home by dinnertime and he wasn't home yet.

What is it called when a father questions a child about a broken window?

A pop quiz.

What is a child?

Someone who stands between his father and the TV set.

Who named the little Egyptian?

His mummy.

Proud mother was always bragging about her year-old son. "And he has been walking since he was nine months old," she told her unimpressed visitor.

"I'd imagine he must be pretty tired by now," the bored neighbor suggested.

What is a definition of a nursery?

A bawlroom.

Father: "Son, what do you want to do when you grow up?"

Son: "I want to drive an earth mover, Dad."

Father: "I'd never be one to stand in your way."

Once upon a time a child became quite upset with her family and decided to run away into the forest. However, she discovered she could not run more than halfway into the woods. Why was this?

More than halfway, and she was coming out of the forest.

Do you believe in clubs for children?

Only when all else fails.

Why did the girl claim she was a twin?

Her mother had a picture of her when she was two.

The overworked mother had just broken up the third fight of the afternoon. "What started it this time?" she asked her two small sons.

Jim answered quickly. "It all started when Todd hit me back."

Teacher to grubby youngster: "What is water?"

Grubby youngster: "A colorless liquid that turns black the minute I put my hands in it."

Question: "How do you know if you have become an adult?"

Answer: "That's easy. You are an adult when you stop growing everywhere except around your middle."

Father to son: "What did you do with the five dollars Grandmother gave you for Children's Day?"

Son: "Well, I spent some on candy and some on bubble gum, and the rest I spent foolishly."

What two kinds of children get into the most trouble on Children's Day?

Boys and girls.

Tearful Theresa was telling how bad things always were for her. "Why, even when I was a baby, Mother was always pinning things on me!" she cried.

What three letters turn a girl into a woman?

A g e.

Question: Sally complained that her brother Joe had smashed her truck. Why was she the one who got punished?

Answer: Joe broke the truck when Sally cracked him over the head with it.

Which child in a family is usually the ring-leader?

The first one into the bathtub.

Do you know the answer? For an active child cleanliness is next to __?__.

(Impossible!)

When a baby is taking a bath, what animal is the child most like?

A bear.

Why did the proud parents put their pretty young daughter in the refrigerator?

To keep her from becoming spoiled.

Why did Sally manage to get into more trouble than any other kid on the block?

She got up earlier than the other children on her block.

Four-year-old Paul and six-year-old Fred had a question about the birds and bees they wanted to ask their father. After several minutes of trying to decide who should ask, Paul said, "You ask him, Fred. You've known him longer than I have."

Flag Day

Though Americans had celebrated Flag Day for years, it did not become an official holiday of the United States until 1949. In that year President Harry Truman proclaimed June 14 as our nation's Flag Day. Every President since Truman has named the same date as the nation's Flag Day.

The first Flag Day was celebrated in 1877, one hundred years after Congress had passed a resolution authorizing a national flag for the new nation. In 1889 a New York City school held a Flag Day program. The next year several states began requiring schools to raise the flag each school day. Philadelphia has the distinction of being the first city to hold a Flag Day celebration that was not part of a school program. This was on June 14, 1893. Four years later New York ordered that the flag be flown over all public buildings. Soon other cities and states followed suit. Today the display of the flag on public and private buildings is a major part of the Flag Day observance. Modern celebrations often include patriotic programs and speeches as well.

Our flag has had a fascinating history. When the flag resolution was passed in 1777, it required only that the flag have thirteen alternating stripes of red and white and thirteen white stars on a blue field. For years after that, a variety of flags were made and flown. In fact, between 1777 and 1779 some flags appeared with only stripes and no stars.

The story of Betsy Ross is well known. She was said to have shown George Washington and others how to cut a five-pointed star. It is also claimed that she arranged the stars in a circle for our first flag. Nice as the story is, it seems to be just a story and not a fact. The truth is we are not entirely certain how much of the Betsy Ross story is fact and how much is legend. We do know she was the official flag-maker for the Pennsylvania navy.

We know for certain that the Stars and Stripes was carried into battle in the late summer and early fall of 1777. We know for a fact, too, that John Paul Jones's ship *Ranger* was flying a United States flag on February 14, 1778. This was the first United States flag to be given a foreign salute. Nine guns on a French ship were fired in its honor. John Paul Jones was also the first to fly the Stars and Stripes in a naval battle.

When Vermont and Kentucky became states, the flag was changed by adding a star and a stripe for each state. It was later decided that this was going to lead to difficulties as other states joined the Union. Each would want its own star and stripe and the flag would keep growing and growing. In 1818 it was decided that the design of the flag should include thirteen stripes only. A star would be added for each new state.

On the night of September 13, 1814, an American lawyer named Francis Scott Key was being held aboard a British warship. He watched as the vessel shelled the American stronghold of Fort McHenry. After the bombardment, the American flag was still flying in the breeze above the fort. The experience so impressed Key that he wrote a poem about it. Later Key's poem became the words to our national anthem, "The Star-Spangled Banner." Although Key considered himself something of a writer he never wrote anything else that gained as wide acceptance as this poem.

In 1824 the name "Old Glory" was first used as a nickname for our flag.

A popular flag story comes from the Mexican War. In 1846 a flag made from pieces of clothing was hurriedly stitched together so the American army could march in victory behind its flag. Another good story comes from the Civil War. An old woman named Barbara Frietchie is said to have had a Union flag flying. When the Confederates marched into town they fired on her flag. The old woman waved her bullet-riddled flag and defied the soldiers. As a result, General Stonewall Jackson ordered his men to leave the brave woman and her flag alone. Though a well-known poem was written by John Greenleaf Whittier about the event, it probably never happened.

Americans have long been noted for their attempts to have the biggest and best of everything. The honor for having made the largest United States flag seems to belong to a Detroit, Michigan, department store. In 1923 the store displayed an American flag 270 feet long and 90 feet wide.

Which band played longest at the Flag Day celebration?

The one that played "Stars and Stripes Forever."

The sailing ship's captain found himself becalmed in the middle of the sea. Not a breath of air was moving. Quickly he ordered the American flag lowered and run up again, this time upside down. Still no one came to his rescue. Why?

Since there was no breeze to blow the flag, no one could tell it was upside down.

How are the American flag and a gardener who raises bluebells alike?

Both have a field of blue.

Why is the President like "The Star-Spangled Banner"?

They are both our national hims (hymns).

How many flags can you fly from an empty flagpole?

One. After that the pole is no longer empty.

Where are flags found on Flag Day?

That depends upon where they were lost.

What did the flag say to the flagpole on the morning of Flag Day.

Nothing. Flags don't talk.

What touches a flag, yet is never seen?

The wind.

Joe: "Which is your favorite holiday?"

Jim: "Independence Day."

Joe: "Spell it!"

Jim: "On second thought, I like Flag Day better."

How are a flag and a pigeon alike?

Both fly over public buildings.

Why aren't flags flown at night?

They don't have the proper navigational equipment for night flight.

When does Flag Day come before Valentine's Day?

When it's in the dictionary.

Two fellows were enduring the lengthy Flag Day speech as best they could. Finally one leaned over to the other and whispered, "What will you be when this gets over?"

"About a year older than when it began," the other shot back.

Father's Day

Two thousand years ago the Romans celebrated a holiday honoring their dead parents and relatives. Parentalia, as it was called, lasted from February 13 to 22. Graves were decorated, families held reunions, and the long celebration ended with a huge family feast. Though all dead family members were honored, not just fathers, this is the closest holiday from history related to our modern Father's Day.

The beginning of Father's Day as we know it came in 1908. On July 5 of that year a special Father's Day church service was held in Fairmont, West Virginia. The next year Mrs. John Dodd was listening to a Mother's Day service in Spokane, Washington. She decided fathers should be honored, too. Due to her efforts, in 1910 Spokane became the first city to honor fathers. Mrs. Dodd wanted Father's Day to be on June 5, which was her father's birthday. However, the ministers of the city chose the third Sunday in June. Father's Day has moved about from time to time but is now always celebrated on the third Sunday in June.

In 1915 the Chicago Uptown Lions Club sponsored Father's Day. They got other Lions Clubs across the nation to do the same. By 1916 President Wilson was celebrating the holiday. Eight years later President Coolidge suggested the day be celebrated nationally. However, he refused to make it a national holiday, as was Mother's Day. Since 1942 a Father of the Year has been selected each year by the National Father's Day Committee. In spite of all this, it wasn't until 1972 that Father's Day became a lasting day of national celebration. In that year President Richard M. Nixon made Father's Day a national observance.

No matter what they say, the women of America seem better able to get things organized than do men, if Father's Day is any example. Mother's Day became a holiday in record time, compared to Father's Day. Perhaps women's lib is a lot stronger than we have been led to believe!

As with Mother's Day, a flower has been chosen as a symbol for Father's Day. Father's Day flowers have long been roses. White roses indicate one's father is no longer living, while red ones are a symbol for a living father.

Many years ago Mrs. Dodd was asked what she felt the modern Father's Day should include. She suggested the family attend church together on that day. Also, a small gift might be given to the father. Finally, she said, "some tender words you've always longed to say to him" might be spoken to Father on his special day. Sounds like good advice, doesn't it?

What letter do fathers commonly drink?

T.

Bob: "Would Dad feel bad if I gave him an old five-dollar bill instead of a new one?"

Bill: "He would be delighted, since it would be worth four dollars more."

What did Dad get for Father's Day?

The bills for Mom's Mother's Day presents.

What did the long-suffering husband reply when his wife claimed the hot summer weather disagreed with her?

"I don't see how it would dare."

Husband to wife: "Will you love me when I'm old and fat?"

Wife: "Of course I do, darling."

When should Dad apologize to Mom?

When he wants to have the last word.

What did Father do when his small son swallowed his pen?

Used a pencil instead.

Why is it that bald fathers are nearly always cheerful?

They don't let anything get in their hair.

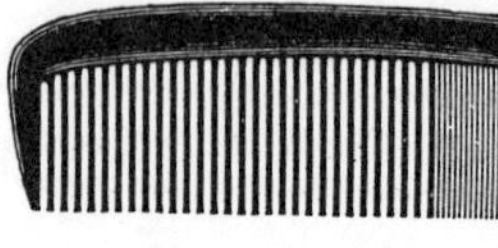

What is it that no man wants, yet no man wants to lose once he has it?

A bald head.

Why is the letter *a* bad for men?

It makes men mean.

Despite equal rights for women, there are two things women can't be. What are they?

Husbands and fathers.

Why did the boy put his father in the refrigerator?

He wanted a cold pop.

What did the bald father say when his son gave him a comb for Father's Day?

"I'll never part with it."

First father: "I run things around my house."

Second father: "So do I. I run the lawn mower, the hedge clippers, the vacuum cleaner . . ."

Joey: "My father is a self-made man."

Bob: "So that's who is to blame!"

Mother to daughter: "What did your father say when he hit his head on the cupboard door?"

Daughter: "Should I say the bad words he used?"

Mother: "Certainly not!"

Daughter: "Then he didn't say a word."

What did Dad do about the annoying noise in the back seat of the family car?

He made his wife ride in the front seat.

Mother: "Why are you crying?"

Son: "Dad fell off the ladder and spilled paint all over himself."

Mother: "Then I'd expect you to laugh instead of cry."

Son: "That's the trouble. I did laugh."

Young Bill just could not seem to behave. Finally he offered to be good for an entire week for a dollar.

"Why can't you just be like your father?" his mother wanted to know. "He is good for nothing!"

Why did the boy say his father was chicken-hearted?

Because he was henpecked.

What two things did Mother say were wrong with Father's dancing?

His feet.

How are a good boy and a naughty boy different?

One does as his father says while the other does as his father did.

Which state is always thought of in connection with fathers?

PA.

Why did the children give their father a large watch for Father's Day?

They wanted him to have a big time on his day.

Independence Day

On July 4, 1776, John Hancock became the first signer of the United States Declaration of Independence. That signing was the result of years of differences between the colonists and Britain. Taxes, government, trade restrictions, and other areas of disagreement had made relations between the two very poor. After the Declaration was signed, there was no question but that war with Britain was certain.

As early as 1770 blood had been shed. On March 5 of that year the Boston Massacre had taken place. Colonists had provoked British soldiers into firing on them. This resulted in the deaths of five American colonists. As a result, relations between colonists and British troops became worse than ever.

On December 16, 1773, the famous Boston Tea Party was held in protest of English taxes. The next year the first Continental Congress met. On April 19, 1775, the battles of Lexington and Concord were fought. Then, on June 15, George Washington became commander of the Continental Army. The Battle of Bunker Hill was fought two days later.

In 1776 the Continental Congress faced the problem of gaining freedom from the mother country. As a result, the Declaration of Independence was written and signed. It was to take years of war before the words of the Declaration would have true meaning. Yet its signing indicated the determination of some daring colonists to convince their fellow Americans that the nation could survive on its own.

The first celebration of Independence Day came the following year. Fireworks, bonfires, and the ringing of bells marked the day in Philadelphia. This was the beginning of the fireworks displays that are so much a part of many modern July Fourth celebrations. Speeches, barbecues, flag displays, rodeos, and parades have been added to the celebration over the years, depending upon the part of the country.

In 1783 Boston began to celebrate July 4. Before that the people of Boston had observed March 5, in memory of the Boston Massacre. During the years following, more and more cities and states began to celebrate Independence Day as their main patriotic holiday.

A number of interesting stories and happenings have become a part of our Independence Day lore. Perhaps the best known has to do with the crack in the Liberty Bell. It first cracked in the 1750s when it was being tested. The bell was repaired not once but twice. Its major crack developed in 1835 when it was rung at the funeral of Chief Justice Marshall. The last time the famous bell rang was in 1846, on Washington's birthday. The strange thing is this famous bell may not even have been rung on July 4, 1776. It was probably rung on July 8, proclaiming the Declaration of Independence.

Perhaps the most interesting July Fourth coincidence has to do with the deaths of Thomas Jefferson and John Adams. Both these great men signed the Declaration of Independence, both were United States Presidents, and both died on July 4, 1826—the fiftieth anniversary of the signing of the Declaration. In 1831 another former President, James Monroe, died on July Fourth. Many people believed these July Fourth deaths were signs rather than coincidences.

Many historic events have been arranged to happen on July Fourth. For example, when new stars are added to the flag, July Fourth is the date when the new United States flags are first flown. Happenings dealing with freedom and communication have often been on July 4. In 1802, on July 4, the United States Military Academy opened at West Point. The Erie Canal was begun July 4, 1817. Our first railroad, the Baltimore and Ohio, was started July 4, 1828. The cornerstone for the Washington Monument was laid on July 4, 1850. The first Pacific Cable was put to use on July 4, 1903, and the Philippine Islands were given their independence on July 4, 1946.

Though several United States Presidents have died on July 4, only one, Calvin Coolidge, was born on July 4.

In the excitement of the day, many forget the true significance of Independence Day. Yet despite the fun and frolic of the celebration, the Fourth of July still remains the outstanding patriotic holiday for Americans everywhere.

What part of his saddle didn't Paul Revere need on his historic ride?

The horn. Traffic was always light that late at night.

What did Paul Revere say at the end of his midnight ride?

"Whoa!"

Which signer of the Declaration of Independence wore the largest shoes?

The one with the biggest feet.

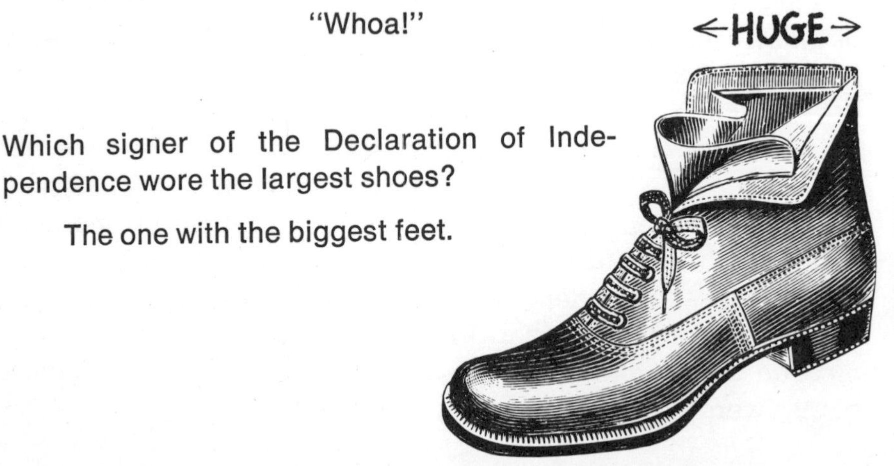

What ghost is seen on the Fourth of July?

The spirit of '76.

When did the Liberty Bell become most like a joke?

When it was cracked.

Everyone recognizes the Statue of Liberty as one of the symbols of our freedom. Exactly why does she stand in New York Harbor?

Because she can't sit down.

Why is the Fourth of July like a chunk of cheese?

It is better with crackers.

Why is a healthy person like the United States?

They both have a sound constitution.

Why did the fireworks committee hope the rain would keep up?

So it wouldn't come down.

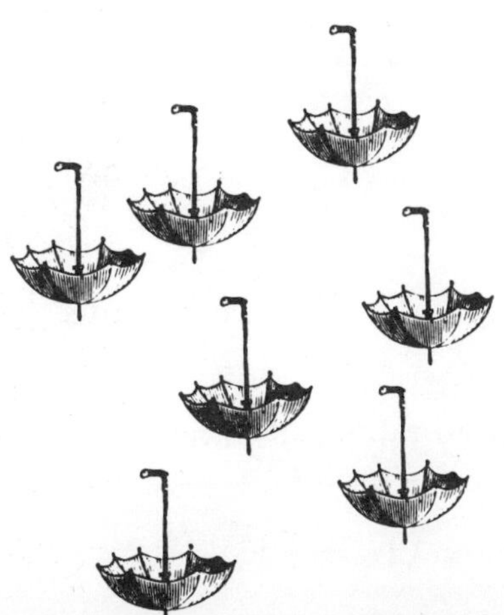

Little Louie was watching the Fourth of July parade from a perch high in a tree. Without warning the branch upon which Louie was sitting snapped, and Louie fell to the ground. The next day Louie, arm in a cast, met Fred.

"Did you break your arm when you fell out of the tree at the parade?" Fred wanted to know.

"Naw," said Louie, "when I landed."

Why did the girl wave her hair for the Fourth of July?

She didn't have a flag.

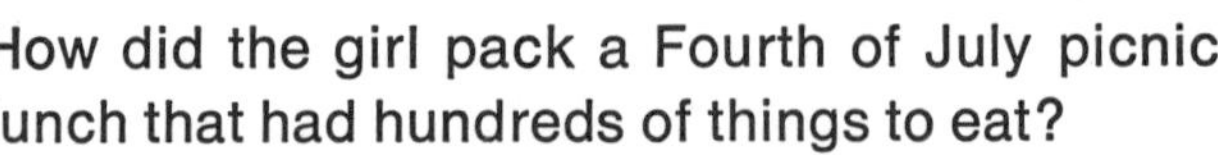

How did the girl pack a Fourth of July picnic lunch that had hundreds of things to eat?

She included a large can of pork and beans.

What do the signers of the Declaration of Independence all have in common?

They are no longer living.

How many nations now have a Fourth of July?

All of them. They have a fifth and a sixth, too!

Labor Day

On the first Monday in September the United States celebrates a holiday that honors the nation's workers. This important holiday is quite logically called Labor Day. Today's celebration means *all* kinds of workers get a day off. When Labor Day first began, it was intended as a holiday only for those workers called the *laboring class.* These were mostly factory workers who were usually overworked and underpaid.

In 1882 Peter J. McGuire was a leader in the Knights of Labor. This was one of the nation's early labor organizations. McGuire was also the president of the United Brotherhood of Carpenters and Joiners. It was McGuire who suggested to other labor leaders that a special day should be set aside for American workers. As a result, America's first Labor Day parade was held on September 5, 1882, in New York's Union Square.

About ten thousand workers marched in that first parade. The rest of their day off was taken up with a picnic, speeches, and fireworks. The idea was so successful the Knights of Labor voted to celebrate Labor Day each year. They set the first Monday in September as a good time, since it came about halfway between Independence Day and Thanksgiving. In 1883 the Federation of Organized Trades and Labor Unions voted to make Labor Day a national holiday.

In 1887 Oregon became the first state to accept the new holiday. Within a few months Colorado, Massachusetts, New Jersey, and New York did the same. In 1894 President Cleveland made Labor Day a legal holiday. The American Federation of Labor set itself the goal of getting as many workers off on Labor Day as were off on Independence Day. This goal was met years ago.

The early Labor Day parades became a time for workers to protest things they felt were unfair about their work. It was common for marchers to carry signs in Labor Day parades. Such signs often read: "Eight Hours Constitute a Day's Work"; "Abolish Convict Labor"; and "All Men Are Born Equal." These slogans said much about the life of the working person in the 1880s in America.

The Labor Day parade is no longer common in the United States. One special Labor Day parade was held in New York City in 1959. Well over a hundred thousand marchers took part and many times that number watched the parade.

Labor Day is celebrated in Europe as well as in the United States. There, however, it is observed on May 1. Speeches and parades are still common parts of the Labor Day celebration in Europe. There the celebration is more apt to be political than it is in the United States. In many ways the European Labor Day on May 1 is very much like our early celebrations of the late 1800s.

Why did the worker always sit on his watch?

So he could be paid for working overtime.

Two men both heard about the same job and both wanted it badly. They got to fighting and in the course of their fight killed one another. Who got the job?

The undertaker.

Who never gets paid for doing a day's work?

The night watchman.

Why did the boss fire his most responsible worker?

Every time something went wrong, that worker was responsible.

"One of these new labor-saving appliances will cut your work in half," the smooth-talking salesman promised the weary housewife.

"Great!" she exclaimed. "I'll take two."

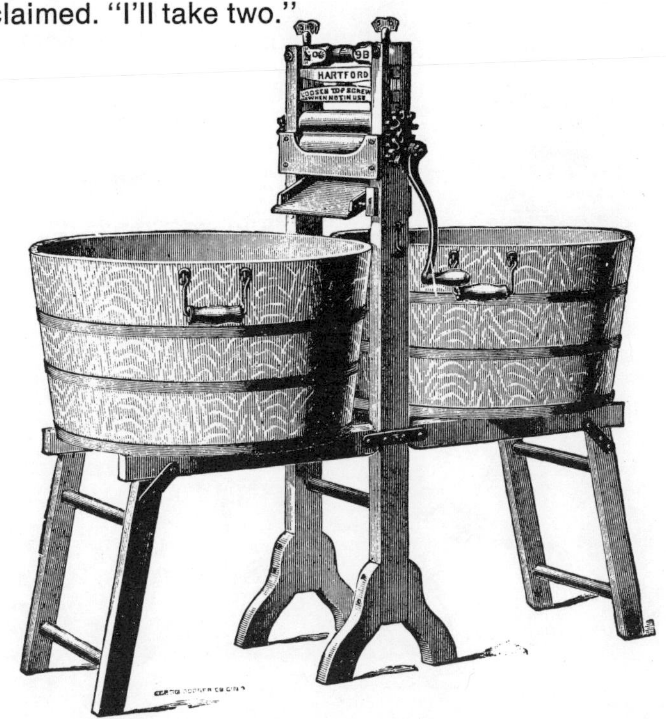

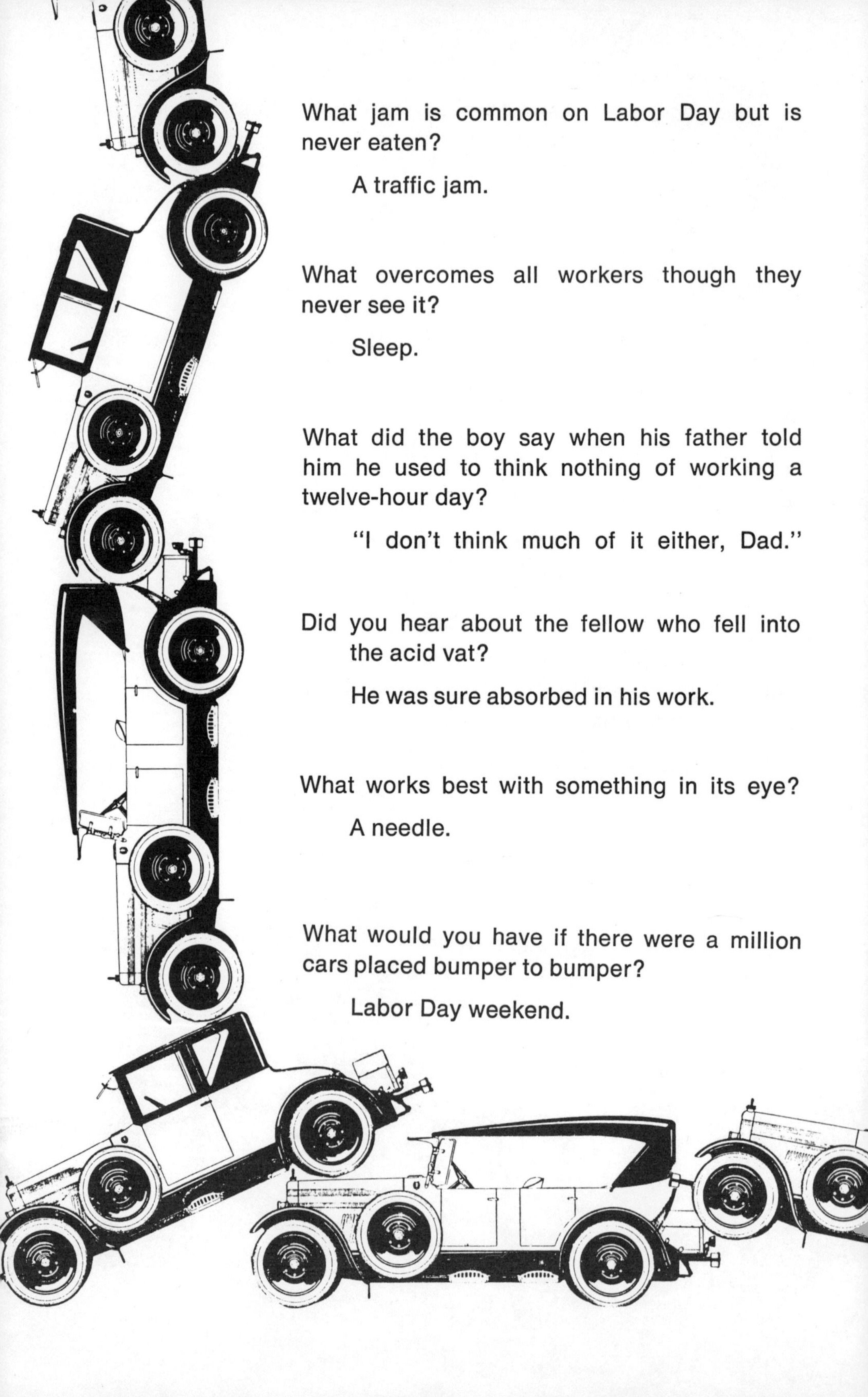

What jam is common on Labor Day but is never eaten?

A traffic jam.

What overcomes all workers though they never see it?

Sleep.

What did the boy say when his father told him he used to think nothing of working a twelve-hour day?

"I don't think much of it either, Dad."

Did you hear about the fellow who fell into the acid vat?

He was sure absorbed in his work.

What works best with something in its eye?

A needle.

What would you have if there were a million cars placed bumper to bumper?

Labor Day weekend.

What is a Labor Day pedestrian?

A motorist who assumed he had gas in his tank.

Sign in an office: Our boss's car is started by a crank.

Sign in another office: You can't beat our boss much as he deserves it.

Sign in yet another office: Right or wrong, she's still the boss.

Which profession always gets back pay?

Chiropractors.

What did the driving instructor tell the student driver when the car's brakes failed?

Aim for something cheap.

The angry boss mailed a lazy employee a notice firing him. A few days later the worker reappeared.

"Didn't you get my letter?" the boss demanded.

"Sure," said his former employee, "but the envelope said return after five days, so here I am."

What is the best place to go if you are short on cash?

To work.

Who is it that usually shows the greatest dedication to hard work?

The boss.

How long had the lazy employee worked in the warehouse?

Ever since the boss threatened to fire him.

How do you make a slow worker fast?

Don't give him time to eat lunch.

Boss to late employee: "What do you mean by crawling into the office?"

Tardy employee: "Well, you said never to walk in late again, sir."

The psychiatrist had treated the patient who thought he was a dog. Finally, after weeks of analysis, the psychiatrist was sure the poor fellow was cured.

"How do you feel now?" the doctor asked.

"Great," was the reply. "Just feel my nose."

What is the best way for a tailor to make a suit coat last?

Make the trousers first.

Why was the pretty nurse named Appendix?

Many of the doctors wanted to take her out.

Why did the abdominal surgeon change jobs?

She hated being inside all the time.

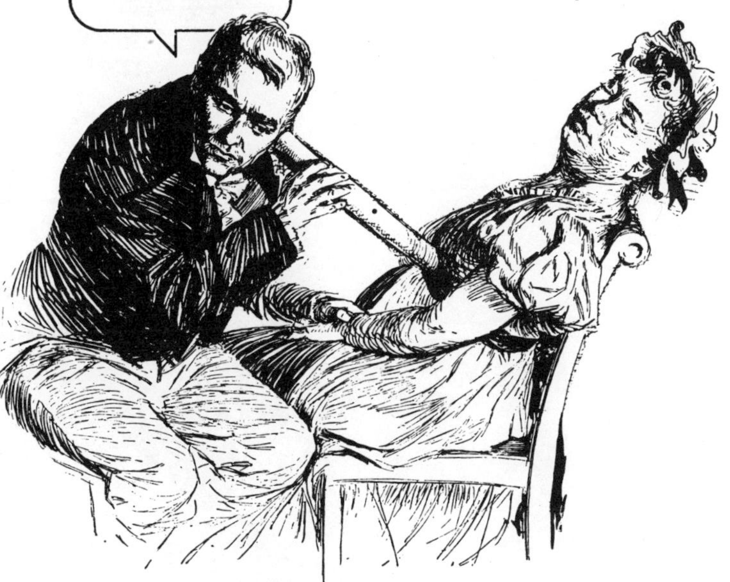

Why did the patient laugh at her doctor after her operation?

Because he kept her in stitches.

Who would you call to help oversee a children's party?

The game warden.

Why did the veterinarian refuse to treat the farmer's ailing hog?

"I would have to kill him before curing him," said the vet.

Why did the professional burglar suddenly switch to robbing coin-operated machines?

He thought the change would be good for him.

Why did the wife of the ferryboat captain make him change jobs?

His work made him cross all the time.

In what business do beginners get to start at the top and work their way down?

Paperhanging.

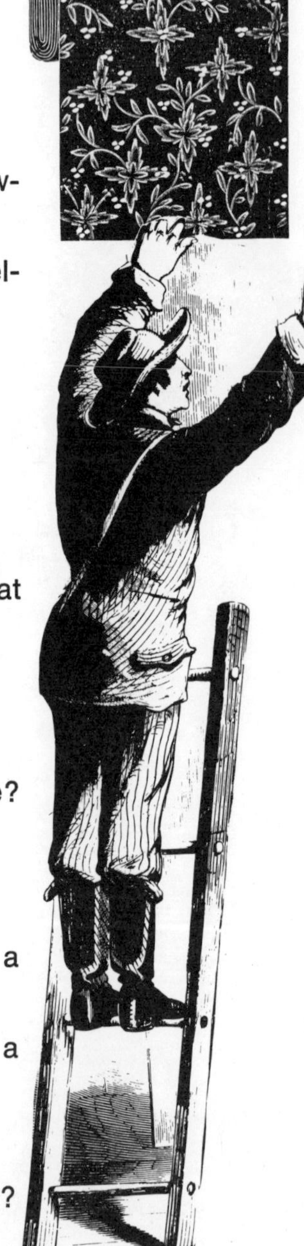

Members of which profession keep on growing forever?

Photographers: they are always developing.

Who always whistles while she works?

The traffic policewoman.

If a ball player gets athlete's foot, what does an astronaut get?

Missile toe.

Why are farmers and authors so much alike?

They both work with plots.

Is it harmful for an author to write on a full stomach?

No, but it is usually better to write on a sheet of paper.

What businessman drives his customers away?

A taxi driver.

Who is the world's strongest worker?

The traffic policeman, who holds up a line of cars and trucks with one hand.

Why was the streetcar conductor late for the Labor Day festivities?

He was thrown in jail for punching a ticket.

How are a dentist and a farmer alike?

They both deal with acres (achers).

Why did the circus hire a six-footer as circus midget?

So they could advertise him as the world's tallest midget.

A manicurist is one who makes money hand over fist.

A waitress is one who thinks money grows on trays.

What do workers do in a watch factory?

Sit around and make faces.

How are a jeweler and a jailor alike?

One sells watches and the other watches cells.

How did the grouchy highway contractor spend his summer?

Building crossroads.

Members of what profession are radioactive?

Disc jockeys.

What workers are counterspies?

Department store detectives.

Joe: "My dentist is a sad fellow."

Friend: "How do you know?"

Joe: "He sure looks down in the mouth every time I visit his office."

Why is an eye doctor like a teacher?

They both examine pupils.

"My daughter thinks she is a chicken," the mother told the psychiatrist.

"How long has this condition existed?" the doctor wanted to know.

"About six years," the good lady admitted.

"Why did you delay so long before coming to me?" demanded the doctor.

"Well, frankly, we needed the eggs," said the mother.

Why do bakers work?

Because they knead dough.

What kept the baker from opening a new bakery?

She couldn't raise the dough.

Why was the weatherman fired?

The climate didn't agree with him.

What worker do we all look up to?

A window-washer on a skyscraper.

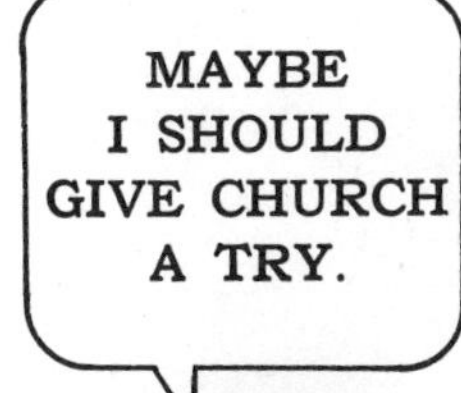

Which worker usually finds things dull?

A knife sharpener.

What do a shoe repairer and a minister have in common?

They both try to save soles.

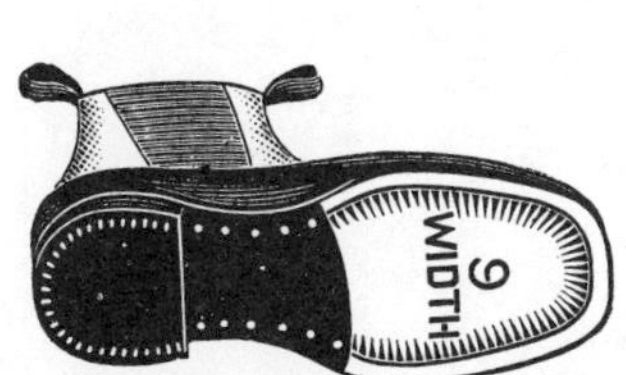

"What happened to your thumb?" asked the doctor.

"I hit the wrong nail," replied the carpenter.

Whose business has the most ups and downs?

The elevator operator's.

Why are cemetery workers considered serious workers?

Because they are generally grave people.

What did the gardener grow who worked in his garden ten hours a day, seven days a week?

Tired.

People from which profession make the best drummers?

Police. They are used to pounding a beat.

Why did the apprentice plumber do such a poor job?

Her boss had looked at the leaking pipe and declared, "This needs fixing badly."

Boss to foreman: "How many people are working this shift?"

Foreman: "Offhand, I'd say about one out of four."

The employer wanted to get his new employee off to a good start. After explaining her job responsibilities, the boss said, "There is one four letter word that I expect from every person on this job."

"What is that?" the shocked woman asked.

"Work!" answered the boss.

A wise old saying—a good boss is one who never puts off till tomorrow what he can get his workers to do today.

In which profession are sound instructors most likely found?

Music teaching.

Why do librarians dislike lending books to bookkeepers?

They never return them.

Did you hear about the actor who left Hollywood because of ill health? His acting made people sick.

Why was the woman with the rumpled skirt hurrying to the cleaners?

She had a pressing appointment.

Why did the power line shock the electrician?

It did not conduct itself properly.

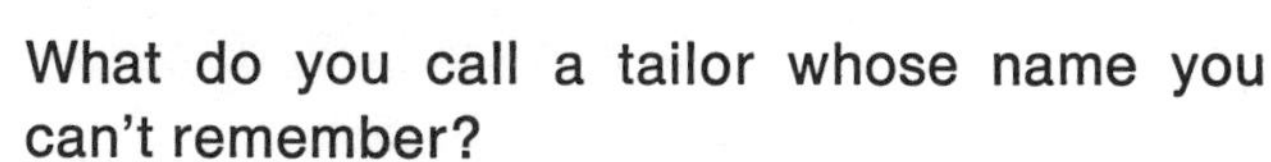

What do you call a tailor whose name you can't remember?

Mr. Sew and Sew.

Why did the tailor complain about business?

It was only sew, sew.

Did you hear about the dentist who married the manicurist?

They have fought tooth and nail ever since.

Mother to child in dentist's chair: "Now be a good boy and open your mouth so the doctor can get his finger back."

Why are dentists like pelicans?

They usually have big bills.

Who can shave twice a day, yet still have a beard?

The barber.

What did the adding machine say to the clerk?

"You can count on me."

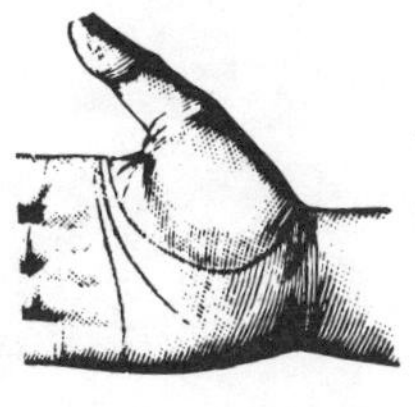

Why did the secretary cut off the fingers on her right hand?

So she could write shorthand.

How can you find an untruthful employer out?

Go to his office when he is not in.

A man returns home after taking a test for a job.

"Were the questions difficult?" his wife asks.

"No, the questions were a snap," says he. "But some of the answers were pretty hard."

Whose business is looking up these days?

The astronomer's.

Columbus Day

October 12, 1792, was the first known observance of Columbus Day. On that day, both in New York City and in Baltimore, Maryland, celebrations were held in honor of the three hundredth anniversary of Columbus's discovery of the New World. The next observance of Columbus Day came one hundred years later, in 1892. In that year a Columbian World Exposition was to be held in Chicago. Actually this "world fair" did not open until 1893, but it set the stage for the celebration of Columbus Day by making people aware of the importance of Columbus's place in history.

Colorado's governor in 1905 asked that the state's citizens honor Columbus. Chicago did the same in 1906. New York State followed in 1909. However, it wasn't until 1937 that President Franklin Roosevelt proclaimed October 12 as a national holiday.

Columbus was born in Genoa, Italy, probably in 1451. By the age of fourteen he had become a sailor, and the sea was important to him from then on. Columbus realized the world was round, as had the Greeks centuries before him. He seriously underestimated the size of the earth, which later caused him to think he had reached the Indies rather than the New World.

England, Portugal, and Italy all refused to sponsor his voyage of exploration. In 1486 he met with King Ferdinand and Queen Isabella of Spain. Six years later his voyage was agreed upon. Columbus was to claim lands for Spain as he found them. In return he would receive 10 percent of any riches from such lands and would be called "Admiral of All the Ocean Seas." It is interesting to note that Christopher Columbus was born Cristoforo Colombo, but when he sailed on behalf of Spain his name became Cristóbal Colón, which was the way the Spanish spelled it.

His famous voyage is one of the best-known stories from history. The tragedy of the situation was that Columbus probably never realized he had discovered something far more important than the Indies he had hoped to reach. One of his less-important discoveries was tobacco, which the New World Indians smoked and his crew took back to Europe with them.

Columbus made three additional voyages to the New World. For a number of years he lived in Hispaniola (now the Republic of Haiti and the Dominican Republic), but never in North America. In spite of the honor due him, Columbus was put in prison on one occasion and was taken back to Spain in chains. His failure to make everyone rich caused many Spaniards to turn against him. The Admiral of All the Ocean Seas died in May 1506, two years after returning from his fourth voyage. In spite of some stories, Columbus did not die poor, but he did die without understanding what his discovery was to mean to the world.

Cities and even a nation are named in honor of this explorer. However, the continents he discovered were named not for Columbus but for another explorer—Amerigo Vespucci—who followed. For a time it appeared even the day celebrated in his honor would not bear his name, as Columbus Day was called Discovery Day. Today his discovery is celebrated throughout the New World, as well as in the European nations of Spain and Italy.

Columbus's bones have crossed the seas almost as many times since his death as he did while living. Columbus's first grave was in Valladolid, Spain, where he died. In 1509 his body was moved to the larger city of Seville, in Spain. Then in 1541 his remains were moved to Santo Domingo. Some historians believe Columbus's bones later went to Cuba and still later were sent back to Seville. There is no positive proof of exactly where Columbus is buried today.

Why was Christopher Columbus known as a fuel conservationist?

He got about five thousand miles on a galleon.

Why were the Native Americans here before Columbus?

Because they had reservations.

How do we know Columbus was a curious man?

He went to see.

MADE IN U.S.A.

How did Columbus cheat the Atlantic Ocean on his first voyage?

By double-crossing it.

One of Columbus's sailors fell overboard. Two sharks who had never seen a European circled the hapless sailor.

"What in the world is that?" asked one shark.

"I'm not sure, but I'll bite," said his buddy.

Sailor: "Look at that water, sir. There is more water than I've ever seen."

Columbus: "You haven't seen anything yet, sailor. You're only looking at the top of it."

What did Columbus say to his men at the start of their voyage?

"Get in."

Did you hear about the sailor aboard the *Pinta* who did such a good job of cleaning he even swept the horizon with his telescope?

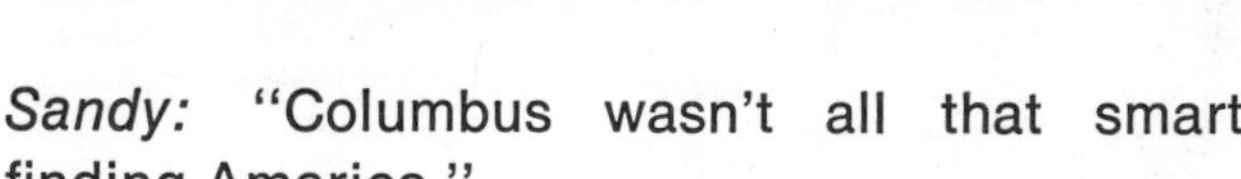

Sandy: "Columbus wasn't all that smart finding America."

Sally: "Why do you say that?"

Sandy: "It is so big it would be hard to miss."

Why did Columbus find the sea so restless at night?

It had rocks in its bed.

Which ships proved most difficult for Columbus?

Hardships.

Why couldn't Columbus's sailors play cards during their voyage?

Columbus always stood on the deck.

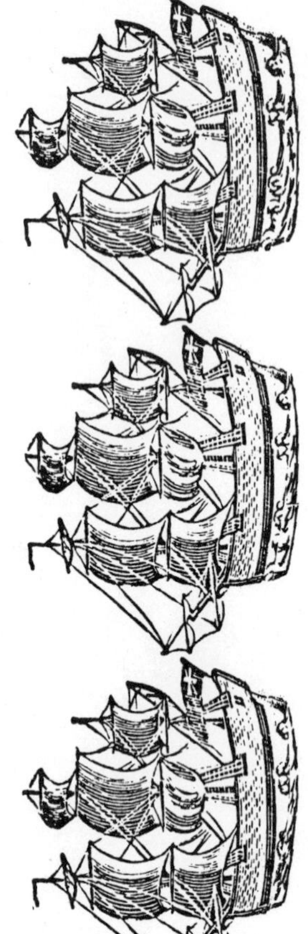

Sailor: "Sir, how close are we to land?"

Columbus: "About two miles, I'd say."

Sailor: "What direction?"

Columbus: "Straight down."

When Columbus discovered America, what did he see on his right hand?

Four fingers and a thumb.

Before Columbus discovered America, how many continents were there?

There were seven, just the same as now.

What did the ocean say as Columbus sailed past?

Nothing. It just waved.

What did the sailor say when he was washed overboard?

"Drop me a line."

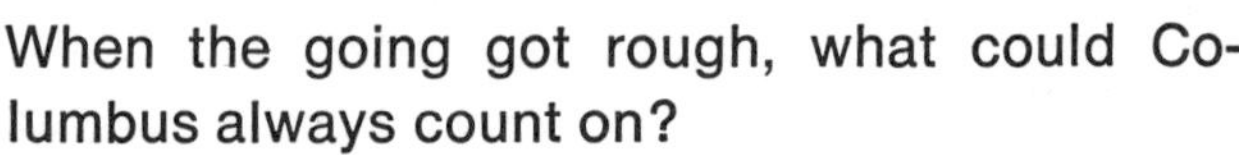

When the going got rough, what could Columbus always count on?

His fingers.

Why did some people think Columbus wasn't very smart?

He didn't know where he was going, where he had been, or where he was when he got there.

Columbus to his ship's cook: "This coffee is terrible. It tastes like mud."

Cook: "That is easy to understand, sir. It was ground this morning."

When were Columbus's ships dishonest?

When they were lying at the wharf.

What did Columbus order thrown out just when he needed it most?

The ship's anchor.

What did the seasick sailor ask the ship's doctor to bring him?

Land.

What did one of Columbus's sailors do when his ship sank?

He grabbed a bar of soap and washed ashore.

Why was the *Santa Maria*'s cook the most unfortunate sailor on the voyage?

He was in a mess all the time.

Which of Columbus's sailors wore the biggest hat?

The one with the biggest head.

What did Columbus have when one of his sailors brought a box of ducks aboard the *Santa Maria*?

A box of quackers.

What did the leaking ship say to Columbus?

"I don't think I can bear you another trip."

When Columbus first landed in the New World, exactly where did he stand?

On his feet.

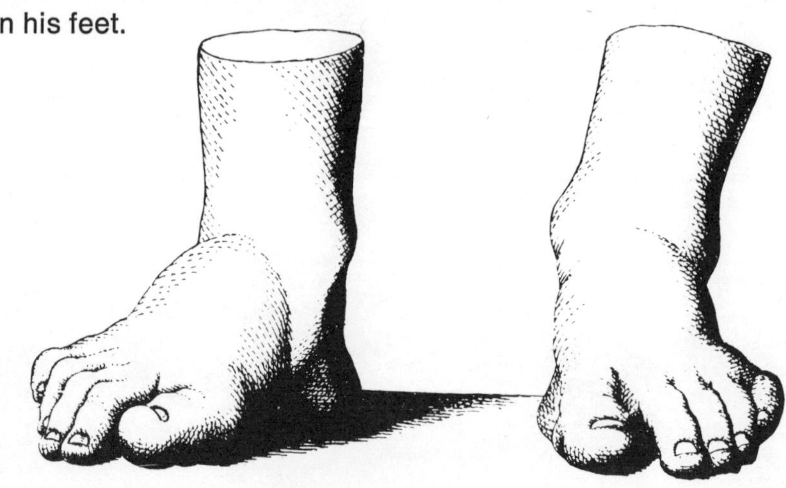

Halloween

We do not know for certain when Halloween was first celebrated. The holiday dates back to the Druids of ancient Britain. For these people November 1 was the New Year and their time to honor the god of the sun. Thus the final night in October became their New Year's Eve. This was the time the dead were thought to come back for a visit with the living. For this reason, people dressed to look like ghosts and spirits, hoping the spirits of the dead would not harm the living.

These people of ancient Britain believed that this was also the time the souls of sinners were forced to enter the bodies of animals. Halloween night became a time of sacrifice to atone for the sins of the dead. Animals and even humans were offered to the gods on that night. Huge fires were built on hilltops to drive away the spirits who came to visit. It was believed that witches danced on the hills while the devil played on bagpipes or used castanets made from the bones of the dead.

When the Romans conquered much of Britain, they put an end to the human sacrifices but not to the celebrations. Ac-

In Scotland, people believed that Halloween was the night when the goblins met to discuss who was to die. If someone went on Halloween to the spot where three roads met, he or she might hear them telling who was soon to die. Should the name of a friend or loved one be heard, the listener could throw the goblins a piece of clothing, which they would take in return for allowing the person named to live a while longer.

People believed that apple peelings and nuts could be used to foretell the future of lovers. A girl could throw a nut into the fire to learn how true her lover really was. If the nut burned steadily, so was his love steady. A nut that burst in the flames indicated a lover who was untrue. A girl could peel an apple skin into one long peeling. If that was whirled around her head and thrown over her left shoulder, it would land in the form of the initials of her true love when it fell. If a girl eats an apple while looking into a mirror on Halloween, she will see the reflection of the one she is to marry as he peeks over her shoulder.

The Irish served mashed potatoes with a ring, a doll, a thimble, and a coin mixed in. The one who got the ring was soon to marry. The one receiving the doll would have children, but the one getting the thimble was doomed never to have a mate. The lucky person finding the coin in his or her food was soon to become rich.

Other Halloween superstitions are just as useful. If a girl carries a mirror in one hand and a candle in the other, she will see the reflection of her lover in the mirror. A fellow who puts nine grains of oats in his mouth and goes walking will marry the girl whose name he first hears spoken. If you eat a dry crust of bread before going to bed on Halloween, your wish will be granted. Finally, if a cat sits beside you, it means good fortune. If a cat rubs against you, it brings good luck; and if it jumps into your lap, that means great good luck.

Halloween costumes come not only from the Druids but from ancient religious festivals in which people dressed to represent saints long dead. Also, masked people were sometimes dressed to stand for the dead. It was their job to lead the ghosts and spirits out of town on Halloween.

One belief about Halloween was that mischief-loving ghosts and spirits played tricks that night. Their Halloween tricks caused all manner of harm and distress. Mischief-loving people soon realized that they could play jokes and pranks on tually the Druids' New Year was the same date as the day on which the Romans honored Pomona, the goddess of orchards.

The Druids' pagan day was eventually adopted by Christians and made All Hallows Day, or a time of honor for the saints of the Church. Hallows Eve or Halloween was a major holiday. From the time of the Druids on, fires played a big part in the celebration. Since ghosts and witches were supposed to be afraid of flames, it was natural to use fire in observance of this celebration.

In Scotland torches were carried into orchards to frighten away witches who were hiding there. Torches were also carried into the fields to make sure of good crops the next year. There were other, more frightening superstitions about fire and Halloween. Bonfires were lighted around rocks that had circles drawn around them. Each rock represented a person. When the fires had cooled the next morning, the rocks were checked. If one person's rock had been moved or had a footprint near it, that person would die before the next Halloween. In Wales everyone threw white stones into Halloween bonfires. If a person's stone was missing the next morning, that person was doomed to death before the next Halloween.

The use of jack-o'-lanterns came from Ireland. There the children hollowed out turnips and potatoes and cut faces into them. Then, just as we do today with pumpkins, a candle was placed inside. This custom came from the tale of a dead Irishman, whose name was Jack. Jack was not welcome in either heaven or hell. In order to light his way as he wandered in search of a resting place, he carried a hollowed-out turnip with a coal from the fires of hell inside.

When is candy not candy?

On Halloween, when it becomes a treat.

What did the trick-or-treater say when she saw the ghost?

Not a word, she just ran.

What did the old witch have that no Hollywood starlet had?

A wart on the end of her nose.

What town is most popular on Halloween?

A ghost town.

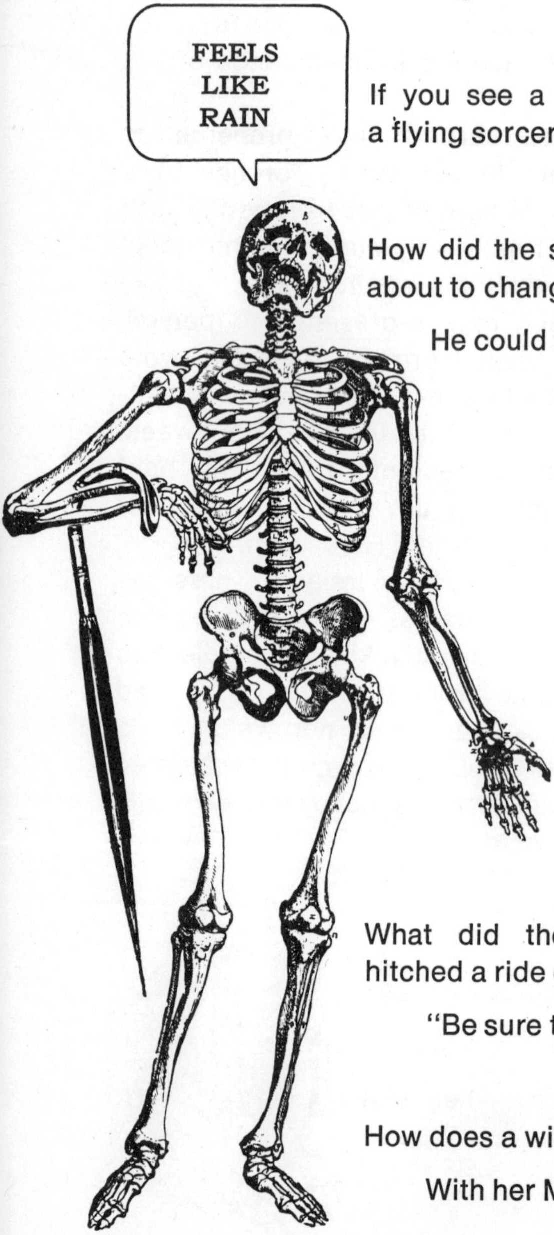

If you see a UFO on Halloween it is likely a flying sorcerer.

How did the skeleton know the weather was about to change?

He could feel it in his bones.

What do ghouls eat?

Things.

What do they drink?

Coke.

Why?

Things go better with Coke.

What did the witch tell the ghost who hitched a ride on her broomstick?

"Be sure to fasten your sheet belt."

How does a witch tell time?

With her Mickey Mouse witch watch.

Goofy: "What is the difference between an apple and an elephant?"

Goofier: "I don't have any idea."

Goofy: "Then you'd better not go trick-or-treating on Halloween."

In what room are you most likely to find a vampire bat on Halloween night?

In the batroom.

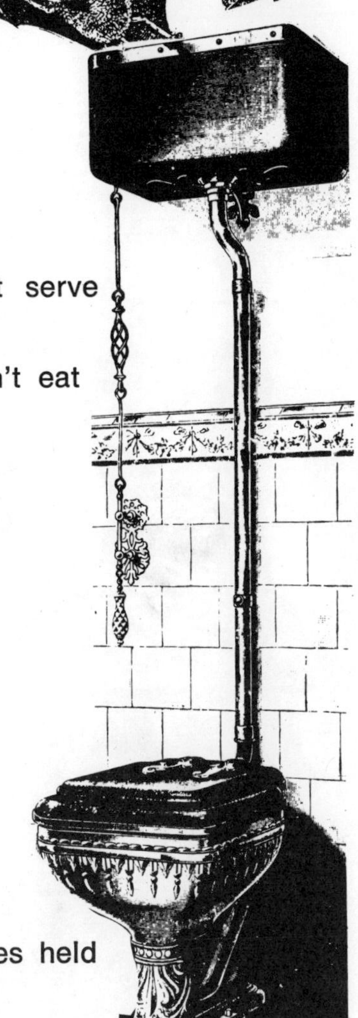

What group guards haunted houses?

The ghost guard.

Waitress: "I'm sorry, but we don't serve witches."

Witch: "That's good, because I don't eat them."

Why doesn't Dracula play baseball?

He won't let anyone use his bat.

"Knock, knock."
"Who's there?"
"Boo!"
"Boo who?"
"Well, don't cry about it."

What happened when the ugly witches held a beauty contest?

Nobody won.

Little Johnny accepted a dare to cross the cemetery at midnight on Halloween. He made the journey in record time and joined his friends with eyes wide.

"I saw a ghost," he panted.

"What was he doing?" the others demanded.

"Well," Johnny admitted, "the last time I saw him he was falling behind fast!"

What do vampires bob for on Halloween?

Adam's apples.

Why don't people believe the lies told by ghosts?

They can see right through them.

What is a vampire?

A pain in the neck.

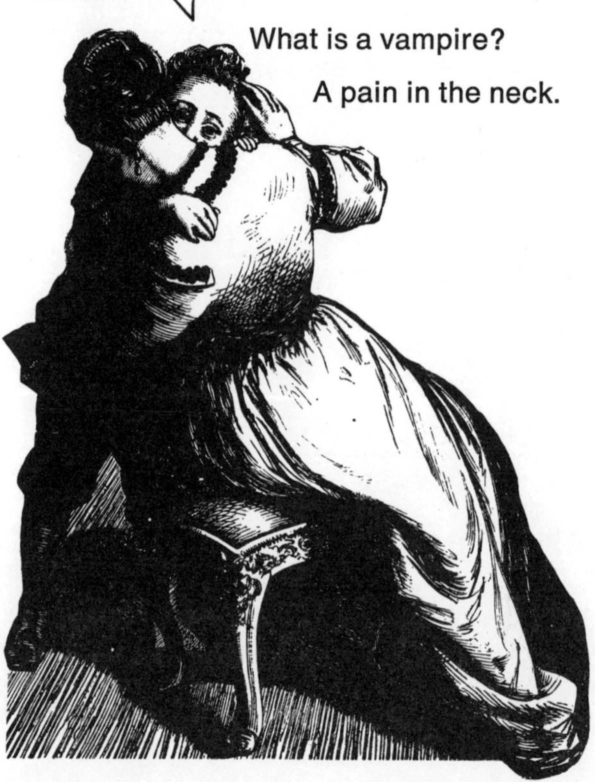

"Knock, knock."
"Who's there?"
"A little trick-or-treater who can't reach the doorbell."

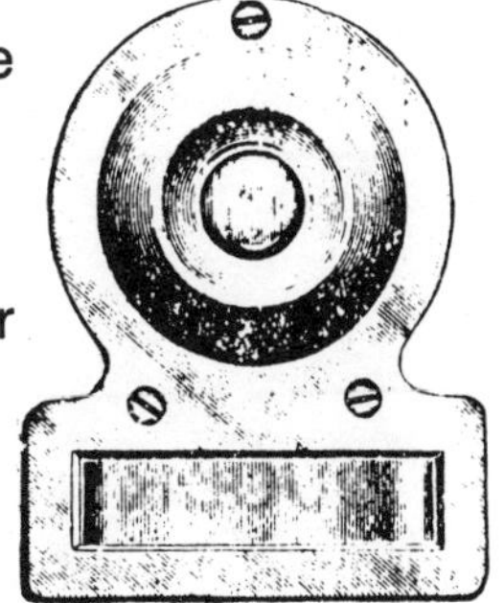

Where do Halloween ghosts receive their mail?

At the dead-letter office.

How did the band of spooks get into the locked cemetery on Halloween?

They used a skeleton key.

If two trick-or-treaters are company and three are a crowd, what are four and five?

Nine.

What living thing has only one hand on Halloween?

An arm.

Why are cemeteries locked on Halloween night?

People are dying to get in.

Why was the young ghost told to mind his table manners?

He was always a goblin.

What did the witch say to her four-footed friend?

"What are you going to wear, wolf?"

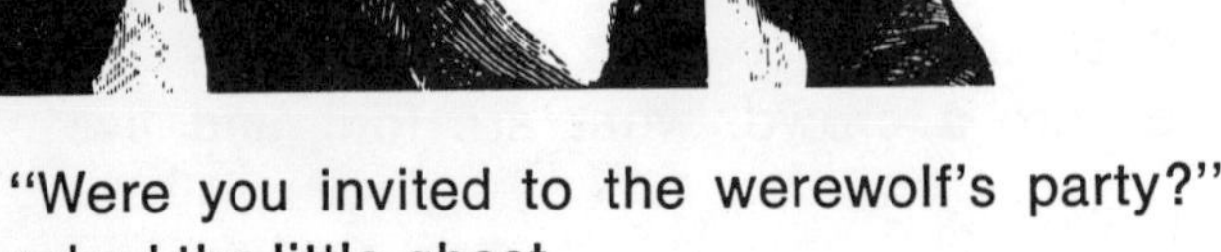

"Were you invited to the werewolf's party?" asked the little ghost.

"No," admitted the other little ghost, "but I hear it was a howling success."

The vampire was poised over his helpless victim. "How do you wish to die?" he demanded.

"Of old age, sir," replied the terrified fellow.

What is a ghost with no sense of humor?

One with a grave outlook.

What is a skeleton?

A bunch of bones with the people taken off.

Why did the spook stay home on Halloween?

He didn't have a haunting license.

On Halloween night what can every witch count on?

Her fingers.

The two ghosts were sitting discussing the world when one asked the other, "By the way, do you believe in human beings?"

Why did the little spook quit courting the girl of his dreams?

He knew he didn't have a ghost of a chance.

What happened when the witch flew her broom into a flock of geese?

She got covered with gooseflesh.

What did Dracula get his son for Halloween?

A black sports coffin.

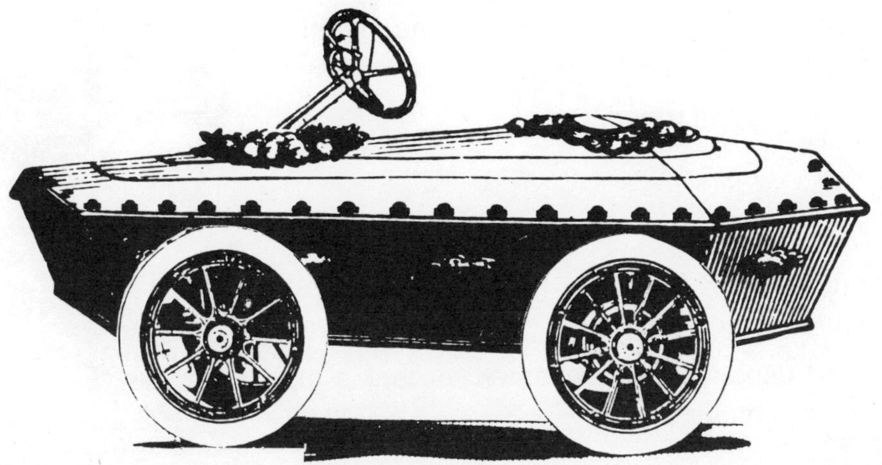

What did the witch say about Dracula?

"He's batty."

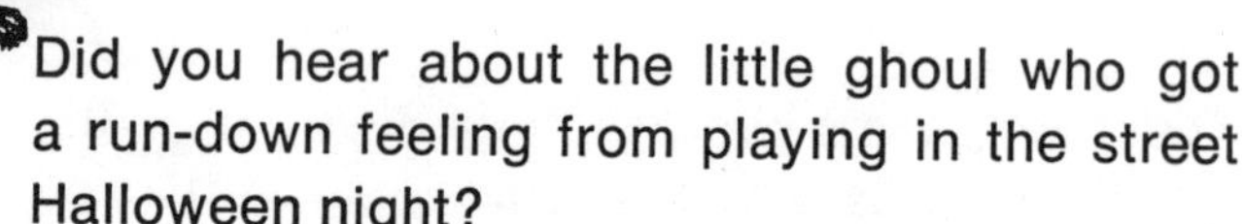

Did you hear about the little ghoul who got a run-down feeling from playing in the street Halloween night?

In her house the witch has six black cats. Each black cat has four black kittens. In all, how many feet are in the house?

Two. Cats have paws.

Who writes the best Halloween stories?

Ghost writers.

What song do ghosts sing on Halloween night?

"A-Haunting We Will Go."

Who did the monster take to the midnight movie on Halloween?

His ghoul friend.

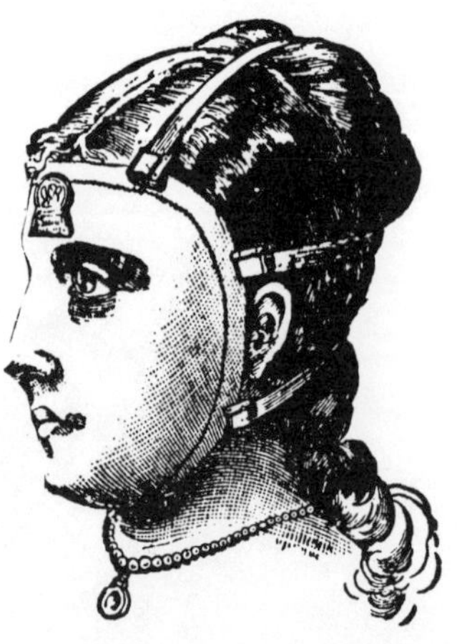

Is it bad luck to have a black cat cross your path on Halloween?

It depends upon whether you are a man or a mouse.

Which witch has her eyes closest together?

The smallest witch, most likely.

What is worse than having a vampire after you on Halloween?

Having two vampires after you.

What is the best way to communicate with a thirsty vampire?

By long distance.

The vampire had a terrible chest cold. What did his fellow ghouls say when they heard the vampire's loud coughs?

"Whose coffin is that?"

How is a ghost like writing paper?

Both come in sheets.

When does one witch become two?

When she is beside herself with anger.

Why do witches ride on brooms?

So they can sweep across the skies.

What is a vampire's average income?

About half an hour before sunrise.

Thanksgiving

In 1621, in Plymouth, Massachusetts, a group of English settlers gathered to give thanks for their survival. The years just passed had been difficult for the Pilgrims. They had left England in 1608 and moved to Holland. Because of difficulties there, in 1620 they set sail for the New World. A leaking ship, bad weather, and ill winds made this journey difficult. Finally, on November 10, 1620, land was sighted. The Pilgrims had hoped to reach Virginia, but they were far off course and had reached what is now Massachusetts.

The aid given the Pilgrims by the Indian Squanto is well known. So are their sufferings during the early days of their colony. When the first Thanksgiving was celebrated, many of the Pilgrim settlers had already died. Yet Thanksgiving was a happy celebration. Ninety or so Indians joined in the three-day observance. Games were played and contests held. Above all, there was plenty to eat. Strangely enough the one food probably not eaten at that first Thanksgiving was turkey, since it was not considered special!

This was the first Thanksgiving as we know it today. However, ancient thanksgiving feasts and celebrations were held by the Chinese, the Greeks, and the Romans. Even the Druids of Britain had a harvest festival, which became the English custom of Harvest Home. At Harvest Home, food from the recent harvest was given to the needy. In some parts of England letters accompanied the gifts of food as a gesture of sharing.

In Europe, beginning in the Middle Ages, a harvest festival was celebrated on November 11. It was called Martinmas in honor of Saint Martin of Tours. Roast goose and new wine have become a traditional part of the celebration of Martinmas. In Germany and the Netherlands, children make jack-o'-lanterns for the holiday; and in part of Switzerland, turnips are hollowed out to hold candles on that day.

The Pilgrims did not celebrate Thanksgiving again until July 20, 1623. For the next hundred and fifty years various colonies observed Thanksgiving or held days of thanks. In 1789 George Washington proclaimed a national celebration of Thanksgiving. He did so again in 1795. Surprisingly, President Jefferson didn't care for the day and did not want it celebrated during the years he was President.

Beginning in 1827 Mrs. Sarah Hale began a one-woman campaign to have Thanksgiving become a national holiday. It wasn't until 1863 that her goal was realized, when President Lincoln issued his Thanksgiving Day Proclamation on October 3. He set the last Thursday in November for the observance. In 1941 President Roosevelt changed the date to the fourth Thursday in November.

We customarily celebrate Thanksgiving with family get-togethers. Today the religious aspect of the holiday—giving thanks to God for our blessings—is not given the importance it once was. Even so, many families still attend Thanksgiving church services. Some large cities have special Thanksgiving Day parades.

Thanksgiving was just a memory while still the turkey lingered on. "How many would like turkey again tonight?" Mom asked.

"What other choices have we?" Dad demanded.

"Just one," said Mother sweetly. "No dinner at all!"

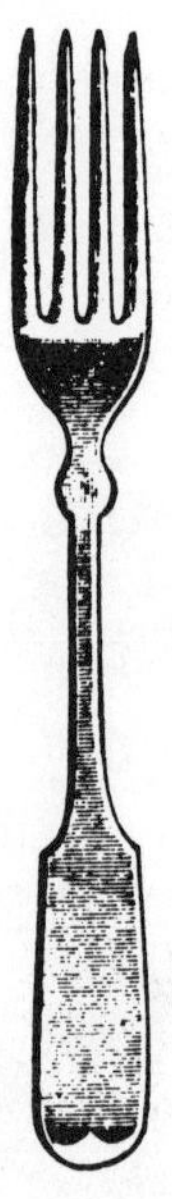

What does everyone want at Thanksgiving, yet work hard to get rid of?

An appetite.

What does a turkey always do when it stands on one leg?

Holds up the other.

What is the most important use for a turkey's skin?

To hold the turkey together.

What nation met an untimely end when Grandmother dropped the Thanksgiving bird?

It was the downfall of Turkey.

What do you lose when you stand up after eating a huge Thanksgiving dinner?

Your lap.

If April showers bring May flowers, what do May flowers bring?

Pilgrims.

Which turkeys have wings, yet can't fly?

Turkey dinners.

Why did the little girl's brother get out of school for Thanksgiving but she didn't?

She was too young to go to school.

How did Squanto change pumpkins into another vegetable for his Pilgrim friends?

He threw them high into the air and they came down squash.

Where did the Pilgrims stand when they landed on Plymouth Rock?

On their feet.

Dandy: "We are having guests for Thanksgiving dinner."

Sandy: "That so? We're having turkey."

What did the Thanksgiving turkey say to the cook?

"I'm too stuffed to eat a thing."

Grandmother: "Well, Tommy, how did you like your Thanksgiving dinner?"

Tommy: "It was fine, Grandmother, only I wish the turkey hadn't eaten so much bread."

How does salt taste best on Thanksgiving?

Sprinkled lightly over turkey.

Christmas

Christmas is, with Easter, chief among Christian religious holidays. Like so many of our holidays, it is celebrated on the date of an old Roman holiday. For a time the pagan holiday and Christmas both shared December 25. Eventually, of course, the celebration of the birth of Christ became the day's only celebration.

Though some groups, such as the Puritans, outlawed the holiday, Christmas has been perhaps our most celebrated holiday. From the time Alabama made it a legal holiday in 1836, it has become official in all states. Christmas is the only religious holiday to be honored in this way.

More customs and beliefs have grown up around the Christmas observance than about any other holiday. Saint Nicholas came to us from Asia Minor, where he died about 350. He was a generous bishop whose memory was celebrated on December 6. Gradually Saint Nicholas became more like Santa Claus and his feast day finally became December 25.

Kriss Kringle came from Germany to Pennsylvania in the 1700s. He, like Saint Nicholas, brought gifts to boys and girls. When Clement Moore wrote his well-loved poem "A Visit from Saint Nicholas" in 1822, it was the beginning of Santa Claus and his reindeer as we now know them. Shortly thereafter Saint Nicholas, Kriss Kringle, and Santa Claus became the same. The only real addition came in the 1930s when Rudolph the Red-nosed Reindeer joined the group.

Christmas carols became popular in the 1800s. Many carols were the result of combining a poem written at one time with music written at a different time. "Silent Night" is one of those carols whose words and music were written at the same time, though by different people. Naturally the idea of caroling followed the popularity of Christmas carols.

The Yule log was intended to be burned every night of the Christmas season until Twelfth Night (January 6). Several superstitions grew up about the Yule log. Some thought its ashes could cure certain diseases. Others felt the sparks from the burning log indicated the number of farm animals that would be born the coming year. When the Yule log is burning, it is bad luck to have a bare-footed person or a flat-footed woman in the room.

The Christmas tree as we know it appeared in Germany in the 1400s. Before that time trees had been used as a part of the worship of many ancient religions. The first Christmas tree in America was written about in 1821. These early trees were decorated with cookies, fruits, and pieces of colored cloth. Not too many years later lighted candles were added and the Christmas tree had become a part of the American Christmas custom.

Of the thousands of Christmas beliefs and customs, here are a few of interest.

Mistletoe was considered a plant of peace. Enemies who met under it could not fight. Besides, kissing is more fun than fighting anytime! It is bad luck to bring Christmas greenery into the house before Christmas Eve. To make fruit trees bear, tie a band of straw around them or beat the tree trunk with a whip on Christmas.

If you bathe on Christmas, you will have boils as a result. On Christmas morning eat a raw egg before anything else, to help you become strong.

A person born during the last hour of Christmas Eve will be able to understand what the animals say. Cattle are able to talk on Christmas Eve and oxen kneel at midnight. Roosters crow at three o'clock on Christmas morning.

An old Scottish belief says that a person born on Christmas has the power to see and command spirits. Those born on Christmas also have the power to predict the future. A baby born on Christmas will be either a lawyer or a thief. If a sick baby is taken to the door on Christmas Eve, Mary will either cure it or take it to join the Christ Child in heaven.

If a young girl puts a bowl of water out to freeze on Christmas Eve, it will reveal the occupation of her future husband. A cake made of flour, water, and salt will cause a girl to dream of her future husband if she eats the cake on Christmas Eve.

Snow on Christmas means Easter will be green. Bread baked on Christmas will never become moldy. Wearing new shoes on Christmas is unlucky. The gates of Paradise are always open on Christmas Eve.

On and on go the beliefs and customs of this most popular of all holidays. So long as people celebrate the day with good will and open hearts, it must bring good for all.

Joe: "Boy, am I glad my dog isn't one of Santa's reindeer."

Sue: "Why?"

Joe: "He doesn't know how to fly."

Why shouldn't you laugh at Santa's fat tummy?

It is not polite to make fun at the expanse of another.

A wise old saying—Christmas is a holiday when neither the past nor the future is as interesting as the present.

How can you drive a car over water on Christmas?

By using a bridge, just as on any other day.

Which of Santa's reindeer should be lightest on his feet?

Dancer.

What did Santa do when people complained his red suit was too loud?

He had Mrs. Claus knit him a muffler to wear with it.

Every day of the year it is filled when you get up and emptied before going to bed. On Christmas it is filled at night and emptied when you get up. What is it?

Your stocking.

A mother sent her young son to the store to buy five pounds of Christmas candy. When he returned home, he had only four pounds of candy. His upset mother phoned the storekeeper.

"Have you checked your scales?" she demanded.

"Have you weighed your boy?" he returned.

Santa looked over the situation and told his reindeer, "It is going to be tough sledding for us tonight."

"How come?" Comet demanded.

"No snow," Santa replied.

How can you double your money just before going Christmas shopping?

By folding it.

What did Santa say when he slid down the hot chimney?

"That burns me up!"

What did the boy say to Santa Claus?

"Drop in and see me sometime."

Which two letters of the alphabet are like a Christmas stocking on Christmas afternoon?

M T.

Why would Santa be like a wild animal if he lost his beard?

He would have a bear face.

Why does Santa wear red suspenders?

To hold his pants up.

Where can you lie on Christmas Eve and still get a present from Santa?

You can lie in bed.

Christmas shopper: "I wish I had money enough to buy a horse."

Friend: "Whatever do you want a horse for?"

Christmas shopper: "Oh, I don't want a horse. Just money enough to buy one."

"I'd like to join your Christmas Club," the young man told the banker. "The only problem is I'm afraid I can't attend some of the club meetings."

Little girl to department store Santa: "And I want a new winter coat."

Santa: "How long?"

Girl: "Why all winter, of course."

Why does Santa call his last stop Fishhook?

Because it is at the end of his line.

Why did the girl beat her young brother up on Christmas morning?

She wanted to see what Santa had left.

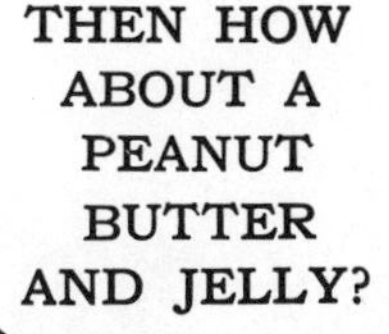

Why didn't the young woman buy Christmas seals?

She didn't know what to feed them.

Why did Santa put "cotton" labels in all the woolen sweaters he gave for Christmas?

To fool the moths.

Little Johnny was the proud possessor of a new Christmas watch. Extending his arm, he showed the present to a friend.

"Does it really tell you the time?" his awed friend asked.

"Don't be silly," Johnny replied. "You have to look at it."

Why is Christmas more likely to have an accident than is Thanksgiving?

Christmas can fall on any day of the week, while Thanksgiving falls only on Thursday.

Why does Santa give toys away?

It would ruin his image if he sold them.

Why did the boy put his bed in the fireplace on Christmas Eve?

He wanted to sleep like a log until Santa came.

Christmas shopper to clerk: "Do you carry refrigerators?"

Clerk: "No, sir. They are much too heavy."

Why did Santa plant a large garden?

He likes to go hoe, hoe, hoe.

Why is a lion in a swimming suit at the beach like Christmas?

Because of his sandy claws.

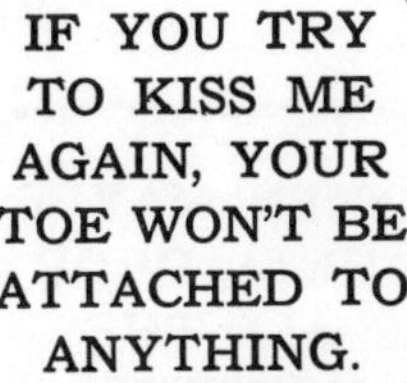

Which toe does not come attached to a foot?

Mistletoe.

One of Santa's reindeer stopped at a lunch counter for a cup of coffee. The counterman, thinking the reindeer wouldn't know the difference, gave him only a quarter in change for the dollar the reindeer put on the counter. Later the man said, "You know, we don't get many reindeer in here."

The reindeer replied, "When coffee is seventy-five cents a cup, I can see why."

Why do elves make toys?

They don't have enough money to buy them.

Why did the children light the fireplace on Christmas Eve?

They wanted to give Santa a warm welcome.

The boy's girl friend had knitted him a pair of yellow and red socks for Christmas. He held them up and asked, "What would they go well with?"

"Very high boots," said his sister immediately.

After visiting the department store Santa, little Lois appeared worried.

"What is the matter?" her mother wanted to know.

"I don't think Santa can read," Lois said, close to tears.

"Why do you say that?" her mother wondered.

"Well, last week I wrote him a letter telling him the presents I wanted and just now he asked me what I wanted for Christmas."

What belongs to Santa, yet is used by boys and girls the world over?

His name.

What do you call a person who has guests for Christmas dinner?

A cannibal.

A wise old saying—Christmas is the time of year when you buy this year's presents with next year's money.

Why do we say Santa kills Christmas Eve?

Because he sleighs it.

Did you hear about the Christmas shopper who broke her leg in the crowded department store?

They gift-wrapped it for free.

What did Santa break just by naming it?

Silence.

Why does Santa go down the chimney?

Because it soots him.

TO

Adams, John, 123
American Federation of Labor, 92, 128
Arbor Day, 86–87
Aztec Indians, 86

Babylon, Ancient, 2
Baden-Powell, Sir Robert, 20, 53
Baltimore and Ohio Railroad, 124
Booth, John Wilkes, 31
Boston Massacre, 122, 123
Boston Tea Party, 122
Boy Scouts, 20–21
Boyce, William D., 20, 21
Braddock, General, 45
Britain, Ancient, 1, 153
Brownie Scouts, 54
Bunker Hill, Battle of, 123
Burbank, Luther, 87

Cadette Girl Scouts, 54
Calendar development, 1, 67–68
Capital, U.S., 45–46
Carnation (flower), 97
Children's Day, 101–102
Chinese festivals, 2, 165
Christmas, 169–171
Civil War, 31
Cleveland, Grover, 128
Columbian World Exposition, 145
Columbus, Christopher, 145–147
Communist countries, May Day parades in, 92
Concord, Battle of, 123
Constitutional Convention, 10, 45
Continental Congress, First, 45, 122, 123
Coolidge, Calvin, 116, 124
Council of Nicaea (325 A.D.), 78
Custis, Martha, 45

Declaration of Independence, 10, 122, 123
Dodd, Mrs. John, 115–116
Douglas, Stephen, 30
Druids, 1, 61–62, 91, 153–154, 165

Easter, 78–80
Egyptians, 1
English customs and the celebration of: April Fool, 68, 69; May Day, 92; Mother's

Day, 97; New Year's Day, 2, 3, 153, 154; Thanksgiving feasts, 165; Valentine's Day, 37
Eostre, 78
Erie Canal, 124
Explorer Scouts, 21

Father's Day, 115–116
Federation of Organized Trades and Labor Unions, 128
Ferdinand, King of Spain, 146
Flag, U.S., history of, 110
Flag Day, 109–111
Floralia, 91
Flower Sunday, 102
Ford, Gerald, 31
Ford's Theater, Washington, D.C., 31
Fourth of July. *See* Independence Day
France: Calendar in, 67; May Day customs, 92–93; New Year's Day customs, 3
Franklin, Benjamin, 8–10
Franklin Institute, Philadelphia, 8
Franklin Typographical Society, 8
French and Indian War, 45
Frietchie, Barbara, 111

German settlers in the U.S., customs of, 15, 79, 170
Germany, 3, 165
Gettysburg Address, 31
Girl Scouts, 53
Gordon, Daisy, 53
Greece, 2
Greeks, Ancient, 1, 165
Groundhog Day, 15–16

Hale, Sarah, 165
Halloween, 153–155
Hancock, John, 122
Harvest Home, 165
Hayes, Pres. Rutherford B., 79

Independence Day, 122–124
India, 68
Ireland, 61–62, 154–155
Iroquois Indians, 2
Isabella, Queen of Spain, 146
Italy, 2

Jackson, Gen. Stonewall, 111
Jarvis, Anna, 96
Jefferson, Thomas, 123, 165
Jones, John Paul, 110
Julian Calendar, 1
Julius Caesar, 2
Junior Girl Scouts, 54

Key, Francis Scott, 110
Knights of Labor, 127, 128

Labor Day, 127–128
Lexington, Battle of, 122
Liberty Bell, 123
Lincoln, Abraham, 29–31, 165
Lincoln, Mary Todd, 30
Lincoln Memorial, 29
Low, Juliette Gordon, 53

Lupercalia, 37

Madison, President, 79
Marshall, John (Chief Justice), 123
Martinmas, 165
May Day, 91–93, 128
McGuire, Peter J., 127
Methodist Church, 102
Mistletoe, 1, 170
Monroe, James, 123
Moore, Clement, 170
Morton, J. Sterling, 86–87
Mother's Day, 96–97
Mount Vernon, 44, 45, 46

Netherlands, 165
New Year's Day, 1–3, 67, 153, 154
Nixon, Richard M., 116

"Old Glory," 110

Pacific Cable, 124
Parentalia, 115
Pennsylvania Gazette, 9
Philippine Islands, 124
Pilgrims, 164, 165
Poor Richard Club, 8
Poor Richard's Almanac, 9
Presbyterian Church, 102
Puritans, 169

Revolutionary War, 45
Roman festivals, 1, 37, 67, 91, 115, 154, 165, 169
Roosevelt, Franklin, 145, 165
Rose (flower), 116
Rose Sunday, 101
Ross, Betsy, 110

Saint Nicholas. *See* Christmas.
St. Patrick's Day, 61–63
St. Valentine's Day, 36–37
Scotland, 13, 68, 154
Senior Girl Scouts, 54
Shamrock, 62
"Star Spangled Banner," 110
Sweden, 92
Switzerland, 3, 92, 165

Thanksgiving, 164–165
Tobacco, 146
Todd, Mary, 30
Tree planting, 86–87
Truman, Harry, 109

U.S. Military Academy, West Point, 124

Valentine. *See* St. Valentine's Day.
Vespucci, Amerigo, 146

Washington, George, 3, 44–46, 123, 165
Washington, Martha Custis, 45
Washington Monument, 46, 124
Weems, Mason Locke, 46
Whittier, John Greenleaf, 111
Wilson, Woodrow, 97, 116

Yugoslavia, 97

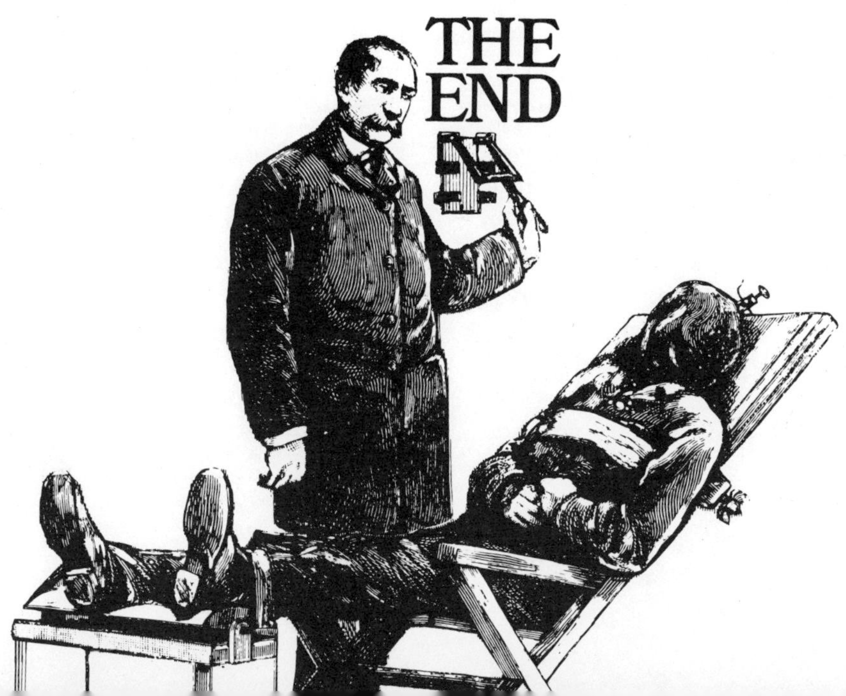

About the Author

E. Richard Churchill is a librarian for the Maplewood Middle School in Greeley, Colorado. For the past seventeen years he has worked as both a teacher and a librarian. This experience with children has made him particularly partial to riddles as a source of fun and teaching reading. Mr. Churchill has over fifteen books to his credit, including *Fun with American History* (Abingdon) and *Puzzle It Out* (Scholastic). *Holiday Hullabaloo! Facts, Jokes, and Riddles* was compiled with the help of his two sons, Eric and Sean, as was his other Watts book *The Six Million Dollar Cucumber.*

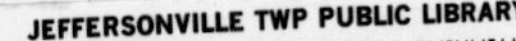